A Reader's Digest Family Music Book

GREAT MUSIC'S GREATEST HITS

97 Unforgettable Classics for Piano and Organ

Editor: William L. Simon
Associates: Mary Kelleher, Elizabeth Mead, Natalie Moreda
Art: Virginia Wells
Research Associates: Penny Larrick, Shirley Miller

Music adapted, arranged and edited by Dan Fox

Annotated by Clair Van Ausdall

Illustrations based on materials from The Granger Collection (pages 178 and 184) and Dover Publications.

THE READER'S DIGEST ASSOCIATION, INC.
Pleasantville, New York / Montreal

Library of Congress Catalog Card Number 79-53751
ISBN 0-89577-066-0

Printed in the United States of America

Introduction

"Try this over on your piano at home," read the sign years ago in music-shop windows, surrounded by several new popular tunes or novelty songs that some publisher wanted you to buy for 15 or 20 cents. "See how it sounds for yourself." "Play what everyone else is playing." Those were magic invitations then, and they still are if you have a piano, if the music has a title you're familiar with, and if you have a few minutes to spare and an imagination full of dreams.

This book of *Great Music's Greatest Hits* offers you an opportunity to play a classical melody on your piano or organ at home as easily as you can play a popular tune.

Most of us have grown up in a world of melody. Whenever we want, we can hear symphonies and concertos, operas and serenades, concert favorites and dances of all kinds, not only in the concert hall and the opera house, but via radio, television and recordings.

But hearing is one thing. Making your own music is quite another entirely. This book of 97 pieces allows you to make the most beautiful music in the easiest way, anytime you feel like it. Here you will find the world's great melodies set down in versions of the original that are playable for a music lover of even modest pianistic attainments. We have chosen the selections carefully, with several specific aims in mind.

First, repertoire. The 97 selections cover a wide range of times and types. For example, there's Bach, who was born in 1685 in a small town in Germany. In this book you'll find some of his church music, some of his teaching pieces, and even some little dances that he wrote to help his new young wife learn to play the harpsichord. At the opposite end of the spectrum is Richard Rodgers, whose last musical, *I Remember Mama*, appeared on Broadway in 1979, shortly before the composer's death at the end of the year. From him comes one of his most beguiling melodies—his version of what royal Siamese children might march to. We also have the great melodists of mid-19th-century Europe—Chopin, Liszt, Mendelssohn—and the magnificent Russians of the late 19th and early 20th centuries who carried piano beyond anything it had ever known—Rachmaninoff, Tchaikovsky, Prokofiev.

Second, arrangements. Many of the pieces were originally created for a symphony orchestra, or an orchestra featuring a solo instrument. We have adapted them into viable solo keyboard arrangements; they are not merely melodies, merely excerpted fragments.

Our arranger, Dan Fox, commented on how excited he was to get a closer glimpse of Sibelius's mysteriously elusive "Valse Triste," to discover how Sibelius transformed his harmonic palette and achieved new and coloristic effects. On the other hand, Dan added, it's equally exciting to discover that the classical composers used basically the same chords, the same chord patterns — the same sticks and stones — to build their "castles" that popular songwriters today use to fashion their "ranch houses." For that reason, Dan has indicated chord symbols above the staves; compare them with a song in another Reader's Digest Songbook, and see if you don't agree with him. (And, of course, if your home-style piano playing is based on chord symbols for the left hand, you can conveniently use them to create your own arrangements of the music we've selected.)

Third, your pleasure. Each of the titles presented here is an entire piece—with a beginning, a middle and an end. And they're all satisfying to play. Play them complete, with all the repeats we've indicated, and you'll have an entrée to each composer's work as he intended it.

Technically, this collection has something for everyone. Many of the arrangements are easy, although a few are fairly difficult. For instance, the Bach "Two-Part Invention No. 1" on page 196 presents quite a challenge if you wish to keep your left and right hands perfectly even and independent, and our version of Gershwin's "Rhapsody in Blue" may require some extra practice.

The organ-pedal notes—those small notes found in the left-hand staves throughout—need not be played on the piano, although if your technique will allow it, they make a nice addition to the richness of the left hand.

We have removed as much elaboration as possible, thus making the result as simple as possible while still preserving the special flavor, style and period feeling of each piece and its composer. You'll feel like a real professional as you play these made-for-you miniatures of the world's masterpieces.

And, best of all **you** *make the music.* There is a special thrill in re-creating a magnificent melody that you have heard and loved for years.

Sergei Rachmaninoff, one of music's legendary pianists and most revered composers, once said that when he sat down at the piano he left one world and entered another. We believe that when you sit down at the keyboard with this fabulous collection of pieces to choose from, your world too will become a different and more beautiful one.

DAN FOX, arranger and composer, graduated from the Manhattan School of Music with both a bachelor's and a master's degree, and studied composition privately with Wallingford Riegger and Vittorio Giannini. Dan's arrangements are familiar through The Reader's Digest Songbooks and some 200 other publications, including performance manuals and song collections for such artists as the Beatles, John Denver, Paul Simon, Elton John, Led Zeppelin and Lawrence Welk. Mr. Fox's "serious" compositions include a symphony, a cantata, an opera and many chamber works. Several years ago, this versatile musician organized a Dixieland-vaudeville band called "The Spirit of '26," which features his arrangements as well as his own guitar and banjo playing. Married to artist June Fox and the father of three children, Dan lives and works in his country house north of New York City.

Index to Sections

Index to Selections

Index to Composers

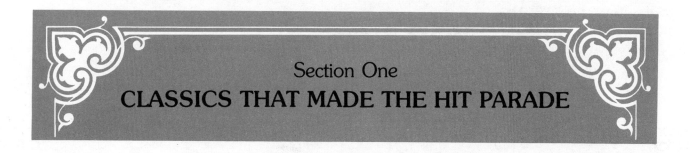

Section One
CLASSICS THAT MADE THE HIT PARADE

Peter Ilyich Tchaikovsky

PIANO CONCERTO No.1

Opening Theme

"Worthless, vulgar, derivative, unplayable." Those were just a few of the adjectives that pianist and conductor Nicholas Rubinstein used to describe Tchaikovsky's Piano Concerto in B-Flat Minor (arranged here in A minor), when he first heard it on Christmas Eve of 1874. Ironically, Tchaikovsky had arranged the piece as a Christmas gift for Rubinstein, to whom he intended to dedicate it. Instead, furious at such treatment,

Tchaikovsky re-dedicated the piece to pianist Hans von Bülow, who was the first to perform it, in Boston, to great acclaim. Within a few years, Rubinstein's distaste for the concerto mellowed, and he became one of its principal interpreters. Of all the work's superb melodies, the most haunting and best known is the opening theme, which, as "Tonight We Love," has become an enduring popular standard.

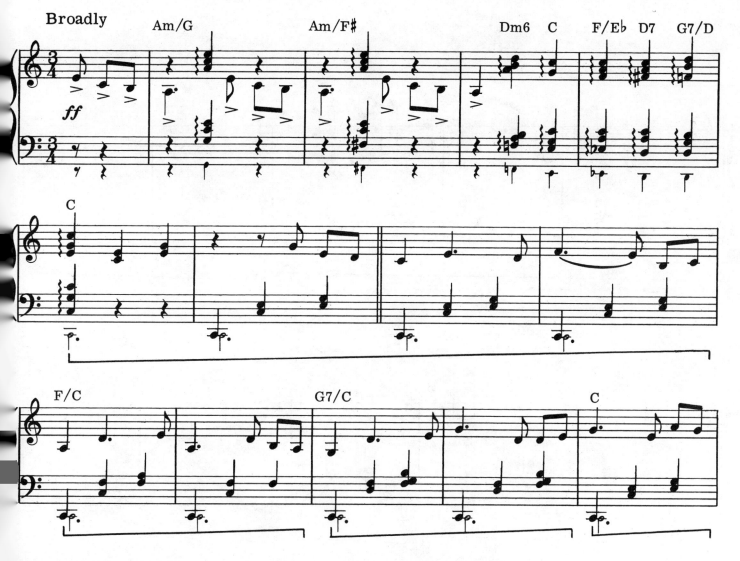

Johann Sebastian Bach

MINUET IN G

from THE ANNA MAGDALENA NOTEBOOK

In 1721, about a year and a half after the death of his much-beloved wife, Johann Sebastian Bach was married again. Anna Magdalena Wilcken, his new bride, was the daughter of the court trumpeter to Leopold, Prince of the German town of Cöthen (Bach served the same prince as Master of Choral Music). Anna sang a great deal, but did not play any keyboard instrument. In the Bach household, where her husband and several of his sons spent hours each day in practice and composition, that was unthinkable. Apparently, Bach set to work to compile a notebook of easy pieces for the clavichord that she could learn—we say "apparently" because some scholars today are not convinced that Bach actually wrote *The Anna Magdalena Notebook*, as the primer is known, for his wife. But, in any event, the minuets, marches and polonaises that make up its content are Bach at his most charming, and they are still favorite teaching pieces. Anna and Johann became one of the happiest of couples, despite the fact that she was only 20 when she married the 36-year-old Bach. How appropriate, then, that Sandy Linzer and Denny Randell turned this Minuet in G from Anna's notebook into a popular song, "A Lover's Concerto," in 1965.

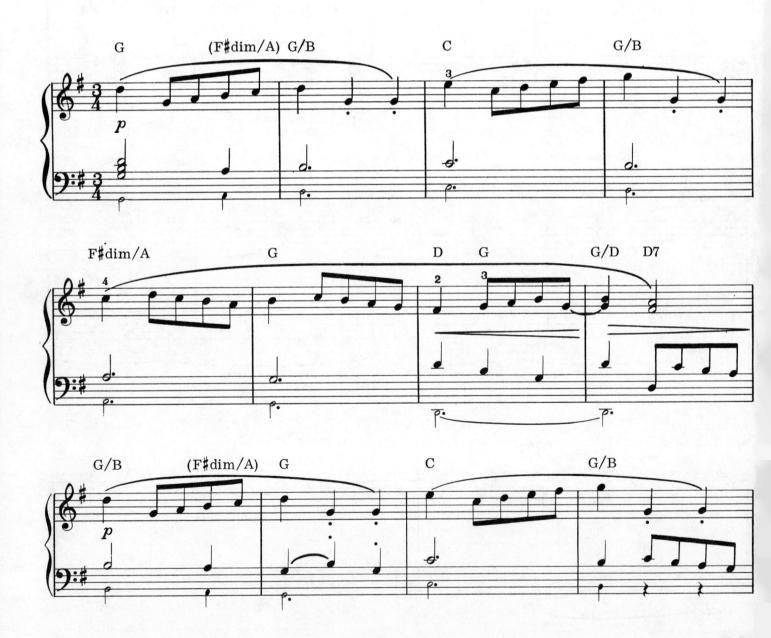

Ludwig van Beethoven

SYMPHONY No. 5

Opening Theme

Beethoven waged constant war with the world he lived in—with his landlords, his debtors, his students, his friends, and, of course, his deafness, the worst of all fates for a composer. Nevertheless, he wrote his celebrated Fifth Symphony in 1805, when he could hear virtually nothing. The work is a triumph—over deafness and all Beethoven's other vicissitudes—and it has become a musical symbol of victory for all the world. It is an outpouring of love, passion, drama, poetry and inspiration, all in music of unsurpassed beauty. In 1976, the symphony's opening notes and its first, febrile theme were given a rock treatment by Walter Murphy, and called, irreverently but wittily, "A Fifth of Beethoven."

Allegro con brio (each measure = 1 beat)

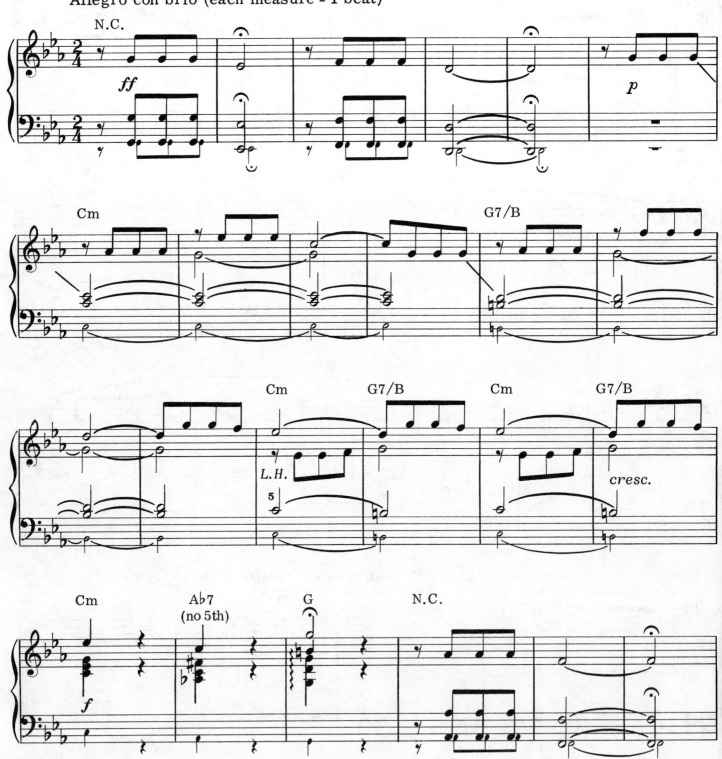

Peter Ilyich Tchaikovsky

SYMPHONY No. 6
(Pathétique)

First Movement Theme

The first performance of Tchaikovsky's Sixth Symphony was only a mild success. By the time of the next performance a few weeks later, which was an unqualified triumph, Tchaikovsky was dead of cholera. He had written for himself a most beautiful epitaph. Its title—"pathetic" —is characteristic of the melancholy composer, who lived in constant fear that his creativeness would one day suddenly dry up. This achingly poignant theme from the first movement was translated into a popular song, "The Story of a Starry Night," in 1941.

12

Sergei Rachmaninoff

PIANO CONCERTO No. 2, Opus 18

First Movement Theme

In his late twenties, Rachmaninoff underwent a depression so severe that he could not play the piano, teach or compose. In desperation he tried daily sessions with Dr. Nikolai Dahl, a psychologist who was doing experimental work in hypnotic therapy. As a result of the treatments, Rachmaninoff began to compose once again. One of his first new works was a masterpiece, the Piano Concerto No. 2. Our arrangement of the first movement theme (which became a popular song, "I Think of You," in 1941) preserves also the eight dramatic chords of the concerto's opening, beginning softly and rising to a shattering climax.

Sergei Rachmaninoff

PIANO CONCERTO No. 2, Opus 18

Second Movement Theme

In gratitude to Dr. Nikolai Dahl for having cured the depression that had prevented him from composing, Rachmaninoff dedicated his Second Piano Concerto to the psychologist. He knew his gesture would be appreciated, for the doctor was a good amateur violist. (On several occasions Dahl had the pleasure of playing in an orchestra that was accompanying "his" concerto.) The lovely melody of the concerto's second movement was made into a pop hit called "All by Myself," by Eric Carmen, in 1975.

Sergei Rachmaninoff

PIANO CONCERTO No. 2, Opus 18

Third Movement Theme

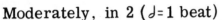

It was Rachmaninoff's compositions that made him world famous at first, but when the composer was forced to leave Russia with his wife and family just before the outbreak of the Revolution, it was with his piano playing that he supported himself. His Second Concerto became his "signature" piece, and to this day it is his most famous large work.

The vaulting theme of the third movement furnished the melody of "Full Moon and Empty Arms," a popular song of the 1940s that captures the poignance and romance of the original and translates it into ballad terms.

Moderately, in 2 (♩=1 beat)

Alexander Borodin
String Quartet No. 2 in D
Scherzo Theme

It took a Broadway musical to make the world aware of one of the most beautiful string quartets ever written. Two of the most popular melodies in the 1953 production of *Kismet* were based on themes from the Russian composer Borodin's Second String Quartet, composed in the 1880s. This melody, the principal one of the quartet's second movement (Scherzo), is the basis for the ever-popular song "Baubles, Bangles and Beads," which provided hit recordings several years apart for such diverse artists as Peggy Lee, The Kirby Stone Four and jazz trumpeter Jonah Jones. A second hit from the same quartet, adapted from the third movement (See Nocturne on page 148), is "And This Is My Beloved," which was sung in *Kismet* by a *vocal* quartet. Pop songwriters also have found glorious romantic themes in chamber music by Tchaikovsky, Schumann and Grieg. And to think that many people are still intimidated by the very idea of string quartets and chamber music in general.

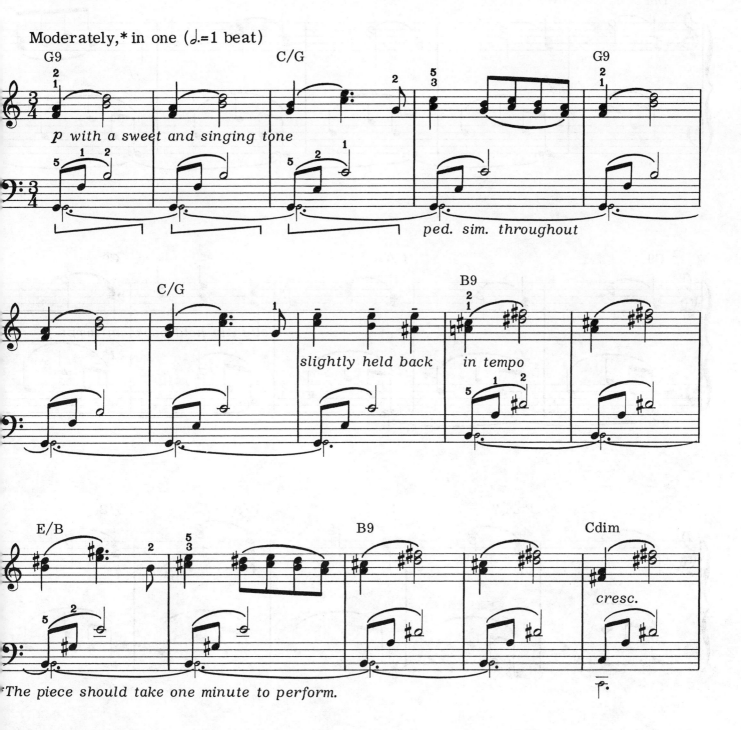

*The piece should take one minute to perform.

Borodin: STRING QUARTET NO. 2 IN D (Scherzo Theme)

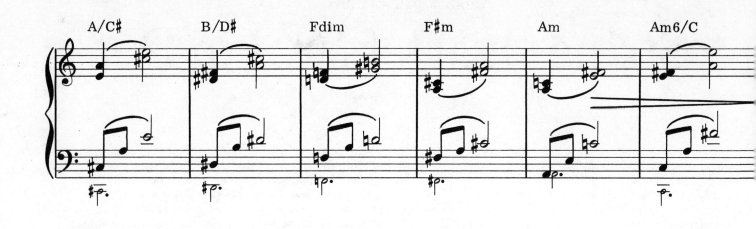

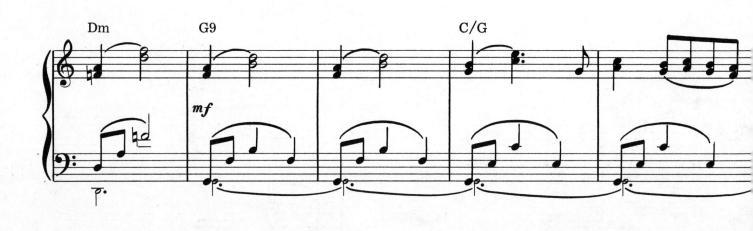

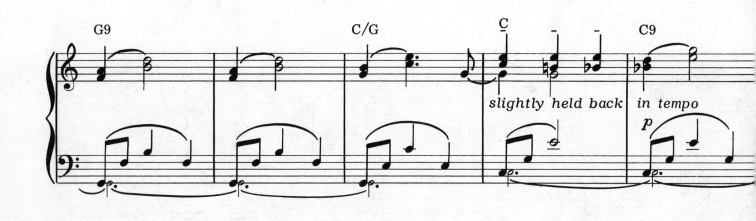

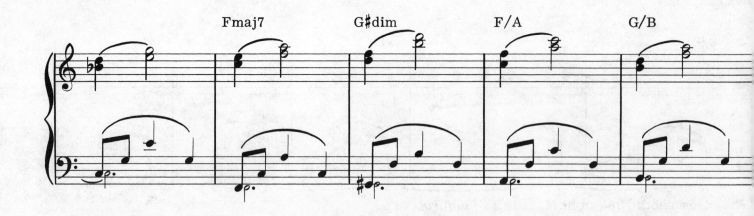

24

8va-⌐

Ludwig van Beethoven

SYMPHONY №.9

Finale: ODE TO JOY

Beethoven, the finest symphonist of his or any time, surpassed himself with the Ninth Symphony, which he began in 1817 and did not finish until 1823. The first three movements, full of shadowy doubts and deliberations, are surmounted by a triumphant fourth movement, which utilizes not only a full symphony orchestra, but a choral ending with four soloists and a huge chorus. Beethoven based the main theme of this movement sometimes called the most perfect melody ever written, on German poet Friedrich von Schiller's "Ode to Joy." The theme is the basis of a hymn with the words "Joyful, joyful, we adore Thee," and of a 1970 pop version called "A Song of Joy."

Peter Ilyich Tchaikovsky

Romeo and Juliet Overture - Fantasy

Love Theme

Shakespeare's *Romeo and Juliet*, so romantic and so tragic, attracted the creative genius of the melancholy Tchaikovsky like a magnet. The composer did not try to tell the story literally in music, but rather fashioned themes that suggest the themes of Shakespeare's play. The love motif, which Tchaikovsky wrote for the melting sound of the French horn, became the melody for "Our Love," a hit for bandleader Larry Clinton in 1939.

Very smoothly

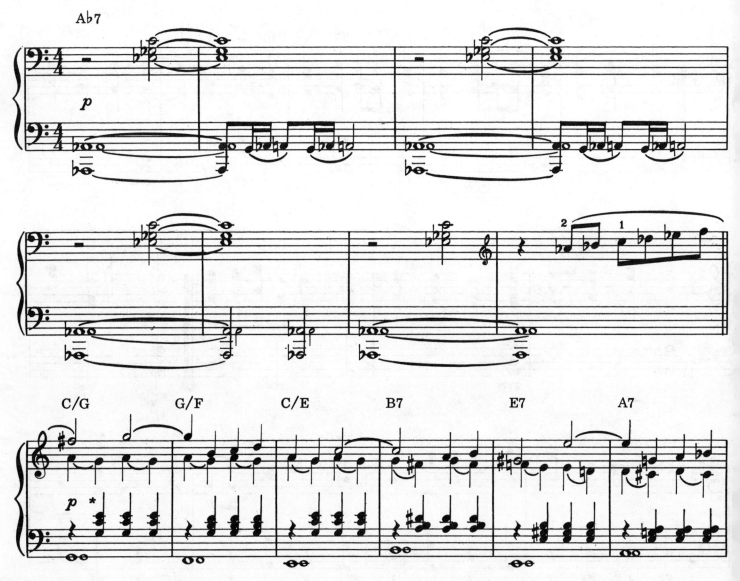

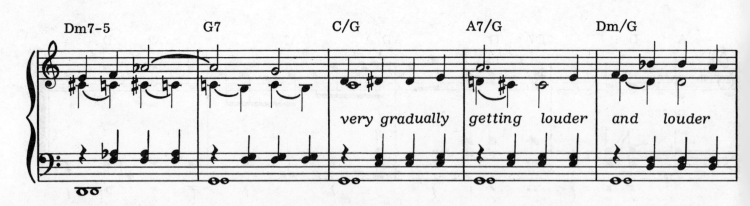

very gradually   getting   louder   and   louder

* *Repeated chords are played firmly and very steadily, but don't pound!*

fading away to nothing

Frédéric Chopin

POLONAISE
Opus 53

(Originally in A flat)

Although he lived most of his pitiably short life in France, Chopin was fiercely proud of being a Pole. Several of his works, including the "Revolutionary Étude," mirror his rage over the harsh treatment his country received at the hands of the Russians, who alternately ransacked and misgoverned it. Other manifestations of his patriotism are found in his polonaises, concert versions of a venerable and stately Polish dance. Chopin added a martial note to the dance, particularly in his most ambitious polonaise, the A-flat major (arranged here in G major), sometimes called the "Heroic." In 1945 Perry Como recorded a pop version of the melody, "Till the End of Time," which became one of the greatest hits of the year.

Chopin: POLONAISE

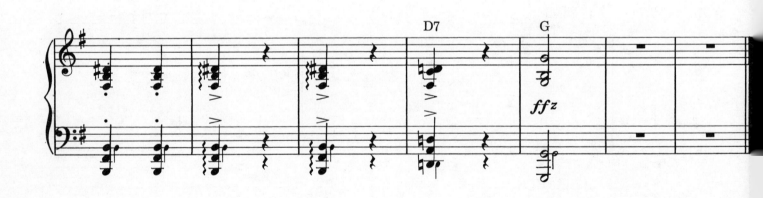

Peter Ilyich Tchaikovsky
MELODIE

For many years Tchaikovsky maintained a deep, productive friendship with a wealthy widow, Mme. Nadejda von Meck. It was a relationship maintained only through letters, however. The two corresponded often and intimately, but, astonishingly, they never met, except once or twice by accident. Occasionally, when Mme. von Meck was absent from her palatial country home, Tchaikovsky would stay there. Following one such visit, he wrote a suite of three pieces for violin and piano, called "Memories of a Beloved Spot." The third of these, "Melodie," has also found fame as a popular song titled "The Things I Love."

Moderately moving, with expression

33

Frédéric Chopin
FANTAISIE-IMPROMPTU, Opus 66

Middle Theme

The "Fantaisie-Impromptu," a whirling bit of pianistic legerdemain with a contrasting dreamy theme of sweetness and naiveté, was among the manuscripts that Chopin's friend Julian Fontana published after the composer's death.

In 1918, this slow, middle theme from the piece became familiar as "I'm Always Chasing Rainbows," which enjoyed a second surge of popularity in the 1930s and '40s, when Tin Pan Alley invaded the domain of classical music in earnest.

Claude Debussy
RÊVERIE

Rather than conventional melodies, Debussy created tonal "impressions," sometimes of landscapes, sometimes of persons, sometimes—as in the case of "Rêverie"—of a state of mind. "Rêverie" was the composer's earliest success, though critics of the 1890s wrote of its "strangeness," "dissonance," "difficulties" and "ugliness," apparently missing the fragile loveliness and vague shimmer which were Debussy's stylistic innovations. In 1939, bandleader Larry Clinton took the piano piece and, calling it "My Reverie," turned it into a popular hit.

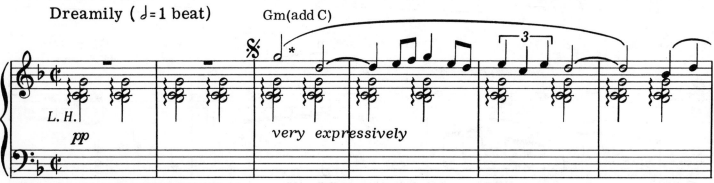

(No organ pedal till bar 11)

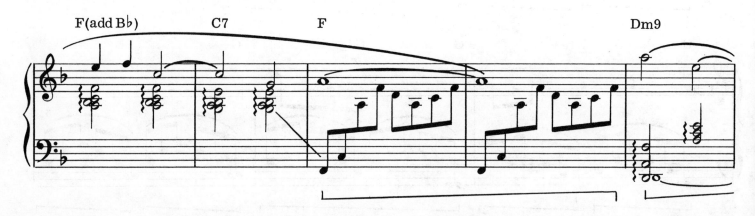

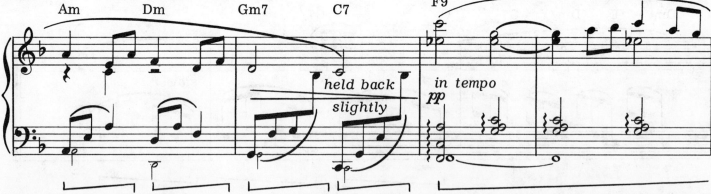

*In this and similar places, top note of left-hand chord should coincide with melody note.

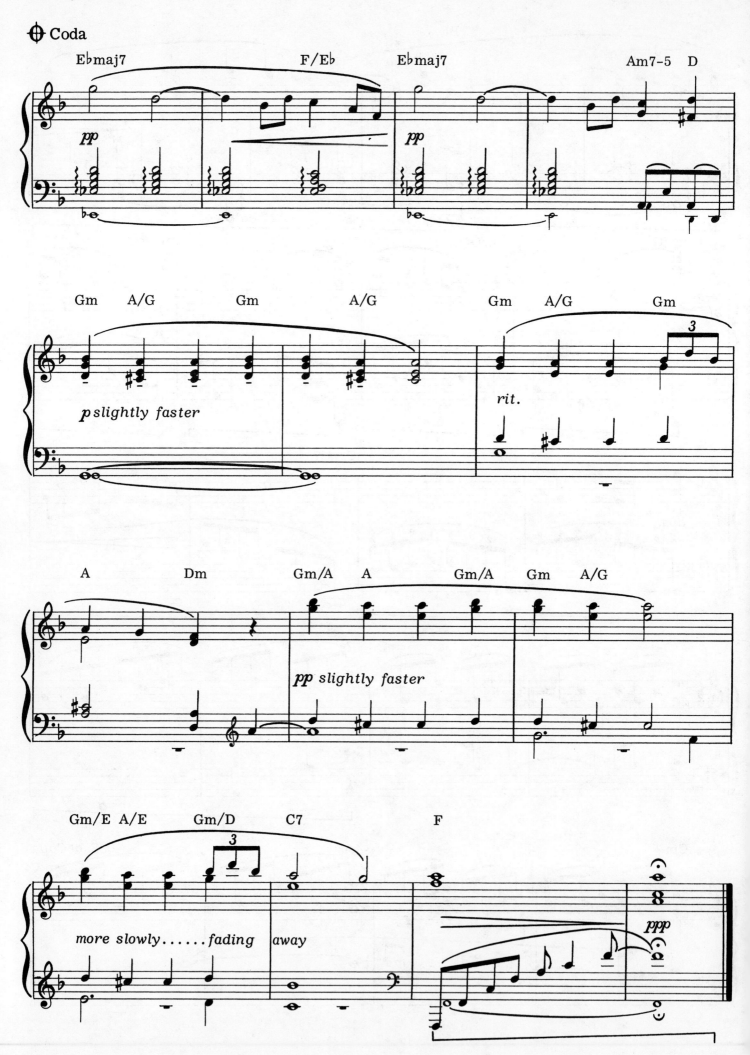

Anton Rubinstein

ROMANCE

Opus 44, No. 1

Anton Rubinstein was hugely successful as a pianist; his fame spread throughout the world, beginning with his first tour at the age of 10. His operas and orchestral compositions were the talk of sophisticated music circles, and the Conservatory he founded in St. Petersburg was the finest in Russia. Today, however, it is the charming little piano pieces he wrote that keep his fame alive. His "Romance," so well known as the popular song "If You Are but a Dream," was originally published in 1868, the first of six short pieces called "Evenings in St. Petersburg."

Slowly, but not dragging

Rubinstein: ROMANCE

Frédéric Chopin

PRELUDE IN C MINOR

Opus 28, No. 20

In 1838, Chopin, with his celebrated companion-nurse Mme. George Sand, journeyed to Majorca to recover his health. However, inclement weather (it was the island's rainy season), his increasing frailness, poor food and lodgings, and Majorcans who either cheated or shunned the composer and the writer turned the trip into a disaster in every way but musically. Despite the rigors of the 3½-month stay, Chopin managed to finish and send to his publisher in Paris the manuscripts for 24 piano preludes. All are magnificent, but the C Minor Prelude, No. 20, has always been especially popular, even before its rebirth as a popular song, arranged by Barry Manilow and entitled "Could It Be Magic," in 1977.

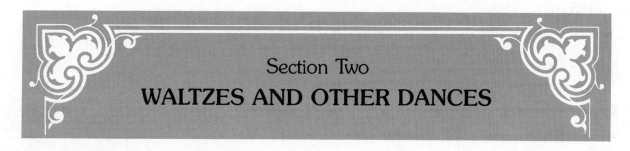

Section Two
WALTZES AND OTHER DANCES

Émile Waldteufel

The Skaters Waltz
(Les Patineurs)

Waldteufel, the Waltz King of France (Johann Strauss, Jr., of course, will always be *the* Waltz King), composed more than 250 waltzes. The dance was the craze of Europe in the mid-1800s—even though it was considered a bit risqué at the time. The composer arranged some of his more popular waltzes for piano solo, so that the bourgeoisie could dance in their parlors while the nobility whirled away in the royal ballrooms. When Waldteufel was appointed director of Court balls in 1865, Parisian society was caught up in the mania not only of waltzing but of ice skating. In "The Skaters," one of his most famous waltzes, Waldteufel capitalized on both those enthusiasms.

Moderate waltz tempo

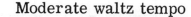

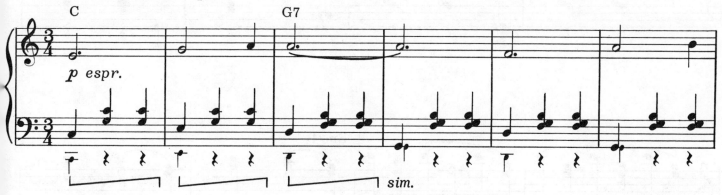

When Johannes Brahms recommended the young Dvořák to his publisher, Fritz August Simrock, it was suggested that Dvořák try his hand at composing something akin to Brahms' hugely successful "Hungarian Dances." Dvořák, from Bohemia, provided a collection of folk-like "Slavonic Dances," which caught the public's fancy immediately. Eight years later, again at Simrock's urging, Dvořák composed another set of dances, and they proved even more successful than the first. This graceful, moody Slavonic Dance in E Minor comes from that second series, which was published in 1886.

Antonín Dvořák

SLAVONIC DANCE, Opus 72, No. 2

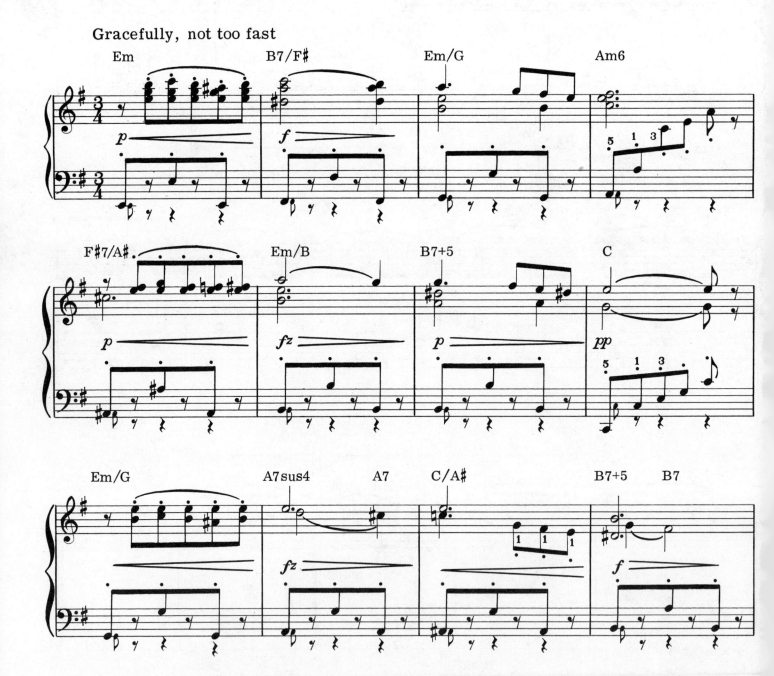

Johann Strauss, Jr.

The Blue Danube Waltz

Although his father wanted him to become a bank clerk, the supremely talented and devastatingly handsome Johann Strauss, Jr., was drawn to music. At the age of 19 he started his own orchestra. Playing music that he himself composed, Strauss soon became the toast of all Vienna, at one point providing orchestras for 14 of the city's café-ballrooms. Evenings found him dashing through Vienna in a cab, stopping at a café here or there, smiling at the dancing patrons, conducting a waltz or two of his own invention, and then whirling off to the next café. "The Blue Danube," the most beautiful and most famous of the more than 500 waltzes he composed, became his signature tune. So popular did the waltz become that, when Strauss visited the United States in 1872, it was arranged that he conduct 20,000 musicians and singers in a mammoth performance of the work at the Boston Peace Jubilee.

Moderate waltz tempo*

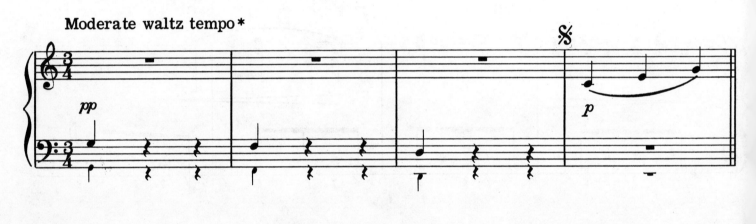

*The second beat of each bar should be anticipated slightly.

50

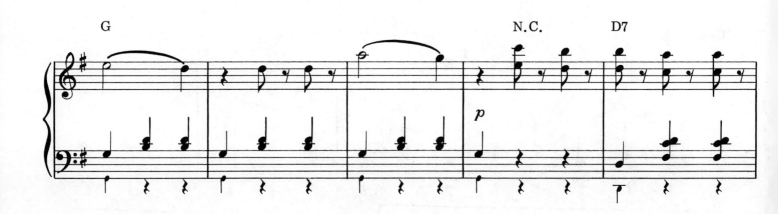

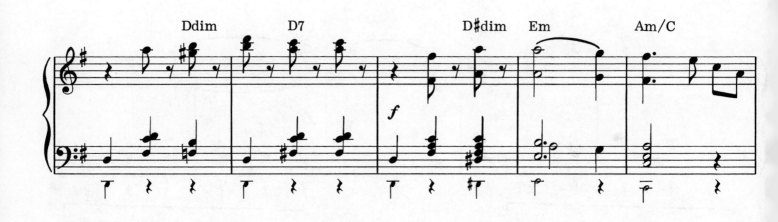

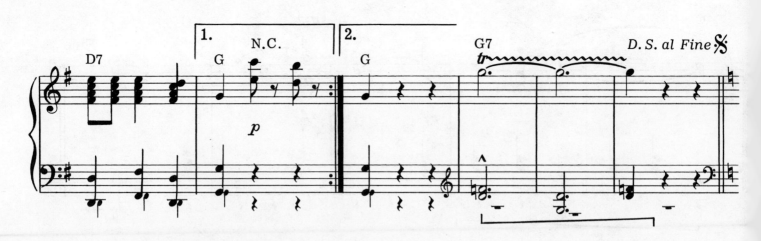

Johannes Brahms
HUNGARIAN DANCE
No. 5

When Brahms published his first set of "Hungarian Dances" for piano in 1869, the tunes became so popular that music lovers everywhere stopped him on the street to beg for his autograph. Brahms acknowledged that most of the melodies for the dances were old gypsy airs that he had learned as a young man, when he accompanied the famous Hungarian violinist Eduard Reményi on concert tours. But stuffy musicologists began to take issue with him over their authenticity. The ensuing fuss in the Viennese newspapers, where musical subjects were often debated in those days, simply helped to promote sales and make Brahms' name even better known. The composer's Hungarian Dance No. 5 is especially gypsyish in its passionate melody and the changes of tempo in the second part (marked "a little slower" and "in tempo" in this version).

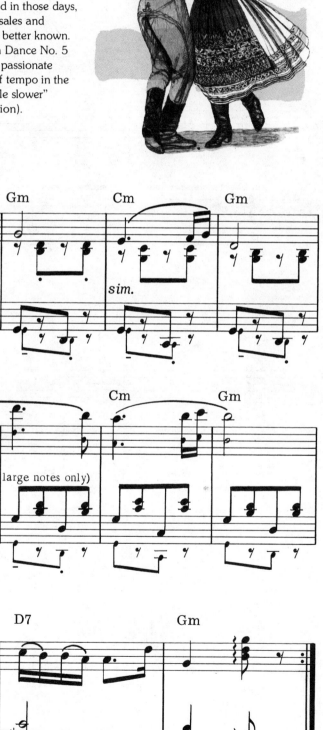

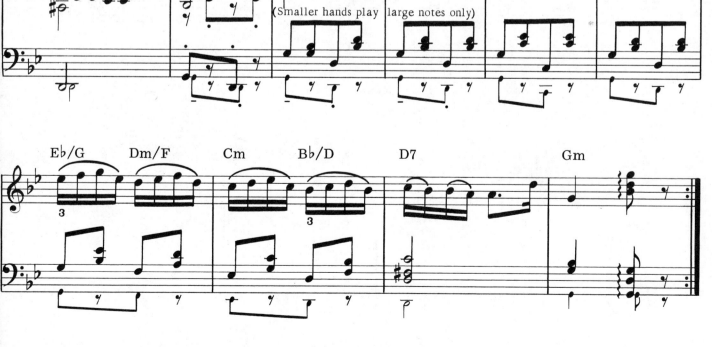

*The second 8th note is tied to the first.

Peter Ilyich Tchaikovsky

Dance of the Sugar Plum Fairy

from THE NUTCRACKER

Stopping in Paris on his way to New York in 1891, to take part in the opening of Carnegie Hall, Tchaikovsky discovered a new musical instrument. It was the celesta, a small keyboard with tiny silver bars that, when struck, sound like exquisite bells. Enchanted, he ordered one to be sent to Moscow in strictest secrecy (lest some other composer discover it and use it first). On his return to Russia, Tchaikovsky, immediately setting to work again on his new ballet *The Nutcracker,* composed the "Dance of the Sugar Plum Fairy," with its enchanting, shimmering phrases for the celesta.

Not too slow

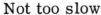

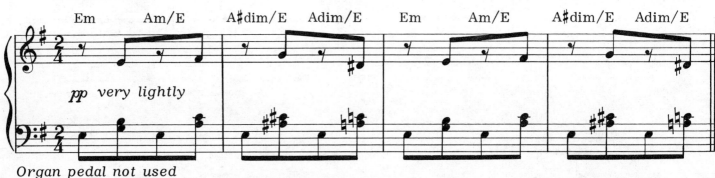

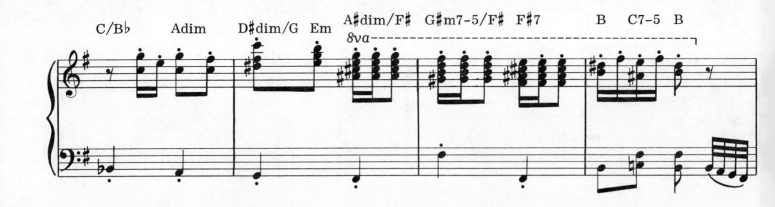

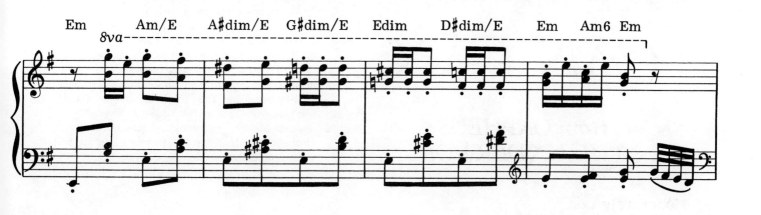

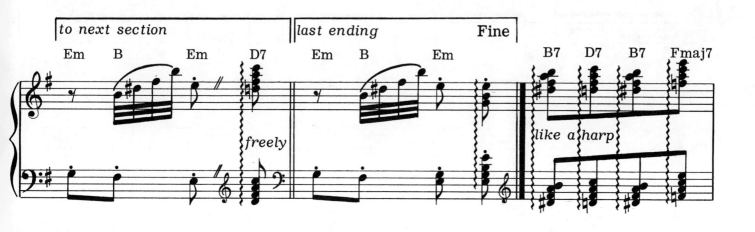

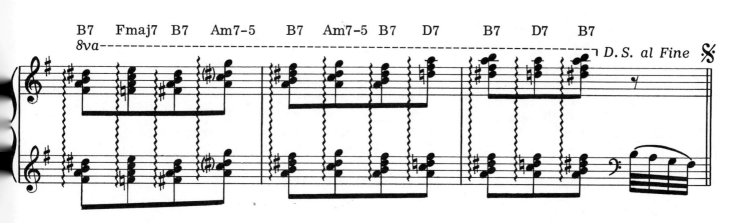

Jacques Offenbach

CAN CAN

from ORPHEUS IN THE UNDERWORLD

Young Offenbach arrived in Paris from Alsace in 1833 with little more than his wits and a big ambition. Within a season or two, he had established his tiny theater as one of the social and musical delights of the city. For it, he wrote operettas so sophisticated and daring that he would not allow his own daughters to attend opening nights. Parisian society was enchanted by the productions. The can-can was the naughty dance that both Offenbach and his audiences loved. His most famous can-can comes from his satirical operetta *Orpheus in the Underworld*, with music so frothy that it seems confected of Parisian gaiety.

Moderately fast

Edvard Grieg

NORWEGIAN DANCE

Opus 35, No. 2

A staunch patriot much beloved by his countrymen, Grieg was one of the first of Norway's composers to seek to create a truly national Norwegian music. Besides his music for Henrik Ibsen's *Peer Gynt*, he composed settings for other Norwegian plays, poems, folk songs and dances. Among the latter was this charming "Norwegian Dance," which he wrote for the piano in 1870.

Manuel de Falla

RITUAL FIRE DANCE

from EL AMOR BRUJO

Manuel de Falla's ballet *El Amor Brujo (Wedded by Witchcraft)* tells the story of a gypsy girl who is haunted by the ghost of her former lover, a jealous but fickle gypsy. In the "Ritual Fire Dance," as fellow gypsies beat with sticks on the kettles and pans they are repairing, she leaps through the flames again and again, daring them to singe her more painfully than love has done. Falla, an Andalusian, was born in Cádiz, where he grew up amid the gypsy melodies and bold rhythms that color his music so uniquely.

*The sign ᴟ means play the written note, the note above, then the written note again.

For example: 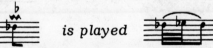 *is played*

By permission of J. and W. Chester/Edition Wilhelm Hansen, London, Limited (for Canada). This arrangement in U.S. Copyright © 1980 Ardee Music Publishing, Inc.

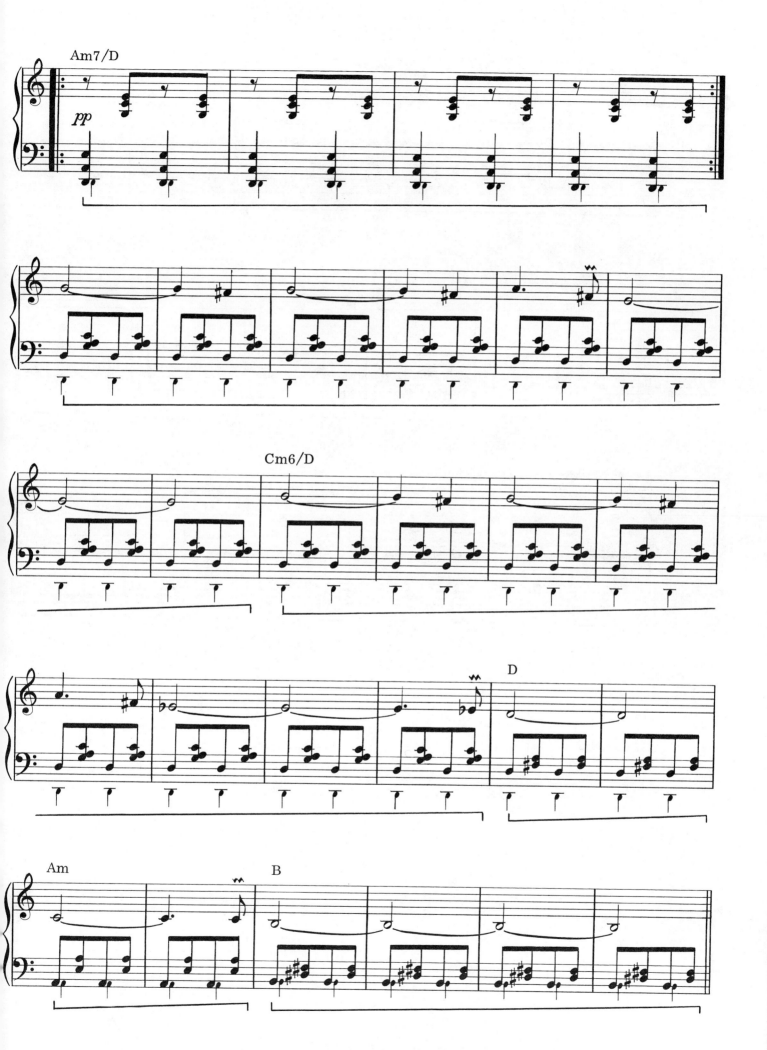

de Falla: RITUAL FIRE DANCE

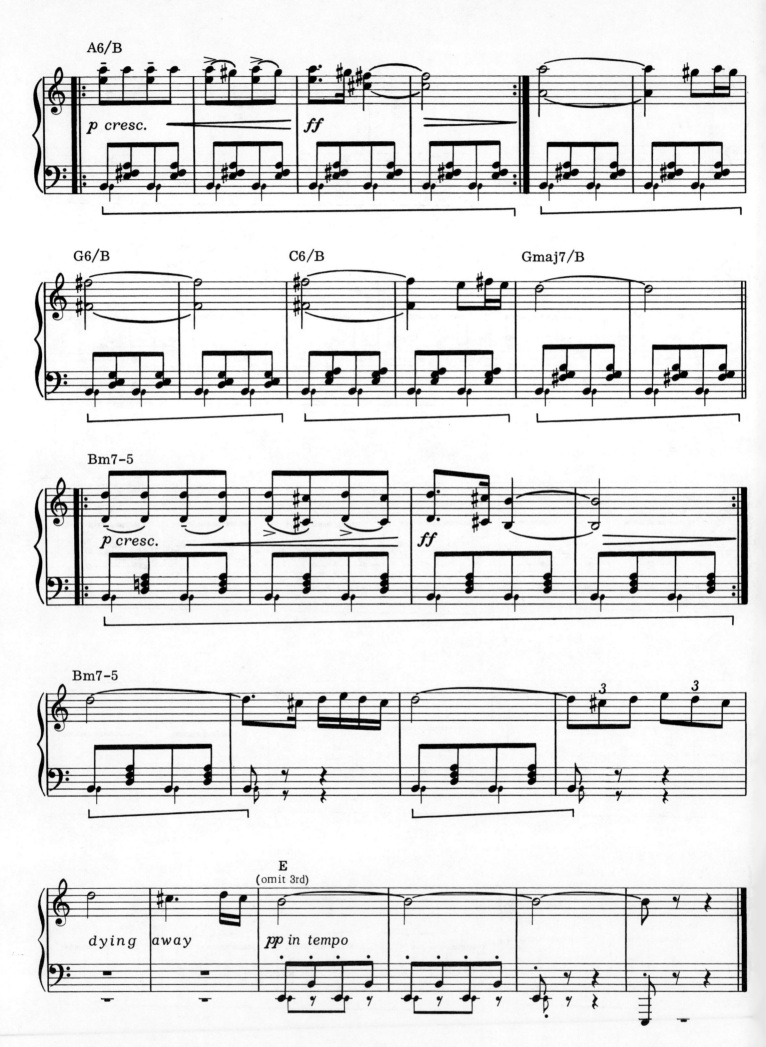

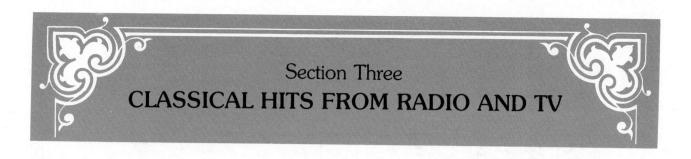

Section Three
CLASSICAL HITS FROM RADIO AND TV

Charles Gounod

FUNERAL MARCH OF A MARIONETTE

Although Gounod had studied to become a priest, he changed his mind at the last minute, and, instead, started composing music for the theater—particularly operas, such as *Faust.* One of his lighter compositions is the mock-heroic "Funeral March of a Marionette," which, with its quaintly menacing melody, Alfred Hitchcock chose as the theme for his TV mystery program. Since Gounod wrote the "Funeral March" for piano rather than orchestra, our arrangement echoes his original impulse.

Very slowly, in 2 (♩.=1 beat)

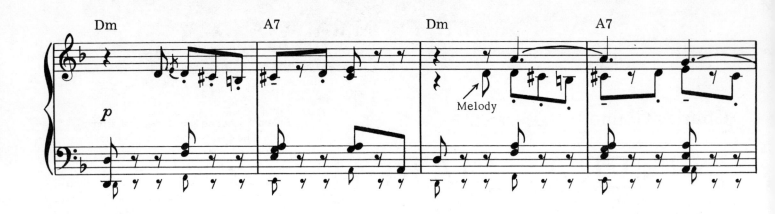

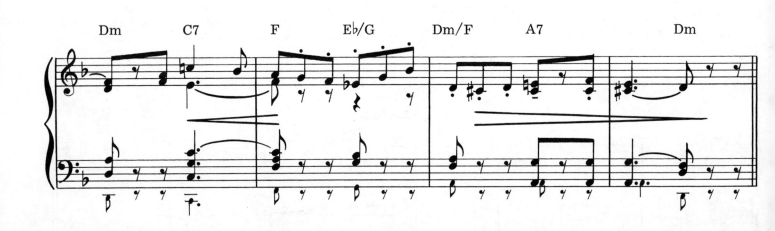

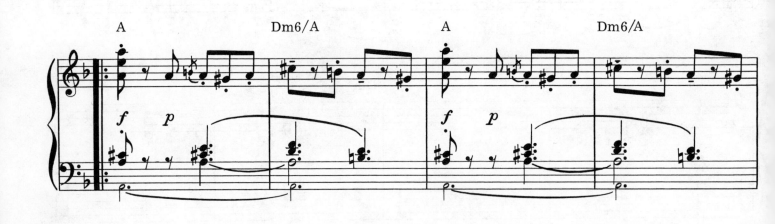

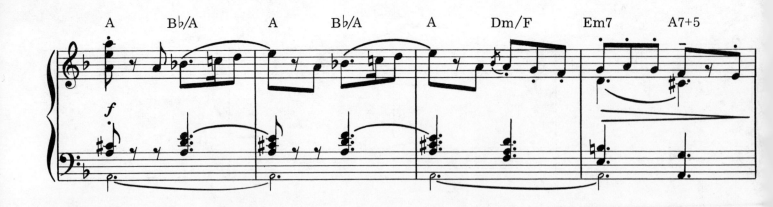

Leroy Anderson

THE SYNCOPATED CLOCK

Before Leroy Anderson chose music as his career, he had intended to become a mathematician, and that interest is evident in pieces like "The Syncopated Clock," which combines a cute melody with a purposely mechanical meter. "Syncopation" means varying a straight rhythm by playing certain notes off the beat. In measure 4, for instance, the third note is played on the second half of the second beat rather than firmly on the third, as we would expect. Similarly, the first note of the first ending is preceded by a rest so that it comes on the second half of the beat. For many years this jaunty theme nightly announced the film on television's *Late Show*, and thus became, with "Blue Tango," "Sleigh Ride" and "Fiddle-Faddle," one of Anderson's best-known tunes.

Rather mechanically

mf (clock imitation)

(Organ pedal tacet till *)

more smoothly

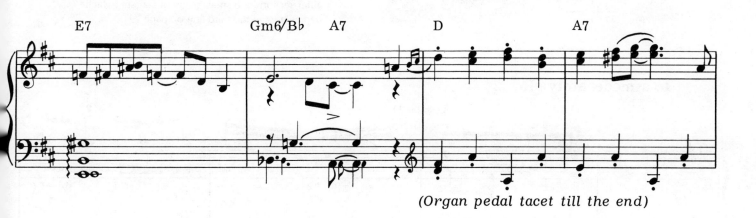

(Organ pedal tacet till the end)

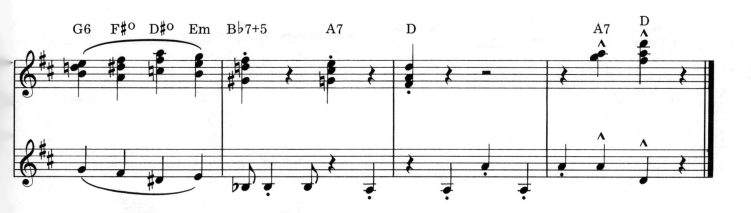

Jean Joseph Mouret

RONDEAU

The name of Jean Joseph Mouret had virtually disappeared into music history books when the producers of TV's *Masterpiece Theatre* selected this piece by the French composer as the show's theme, and brought his name to light once again. Mouret wrote his music in Paris in the early 1700s, when collections of pieces, called "divertissements" —scored for a band of reed instruments, brasses, drums and a few strings—were played at the banquets and other festivities that were indulged in by rich peers like Mouret's patroness, the Duchess of Maine. Mouret based this portion of a divertissement on the rondeau, a type of song of the 13th and 14th centuries that called for a chorus of voices for the refrain and a solo voice for the verse. His instrumental version resembles that early practice, with a main section for full orchestra (played first here), and a contrasting, airier section for a small group of players (which begins here at the third line on page 71).

All trills begin on the note above the written note.

Jean Sibelius

VALSE TRISTE
Opus 44

from KUOLEMA

Sibelius, Finland's most renowned composer, wrote his "Mournful Waltz" as background music for a scene in *Kuolema*, a play by Arvid Jaernefelt. In the play, an aged mother who lies dying believes she sees the figure of Death enter her dim room; moving to an eerie rhythm, he entices her into his arms for a final waltz. The music begins with strange, uneasy chords and a somber melody, but by its end, the mood has become quiet, the harmonies gentle. In 1897, when Sibelius was only 32, the Finnish government awarded him a lifelong pension that permitted him to devote his life to music. This waltz was for many years the theme for the radio show *I Love a Mystery*.

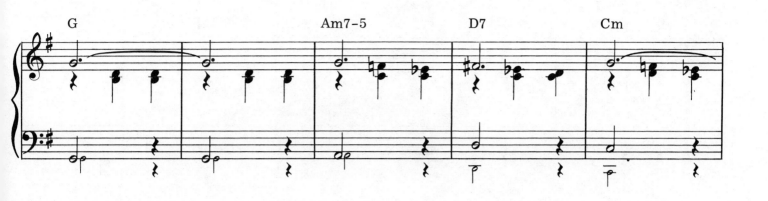

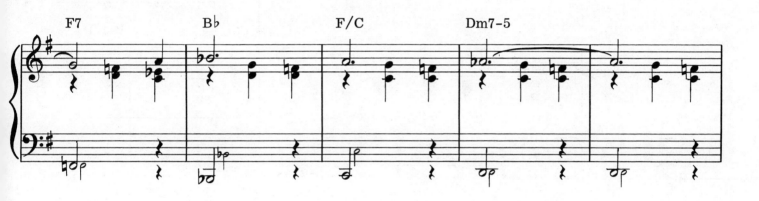

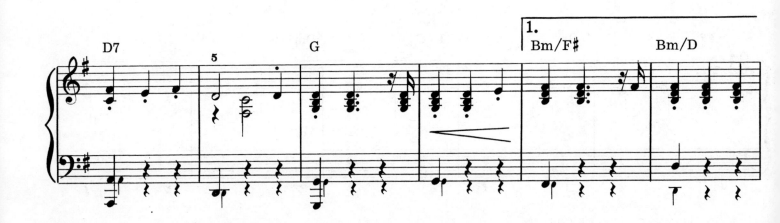

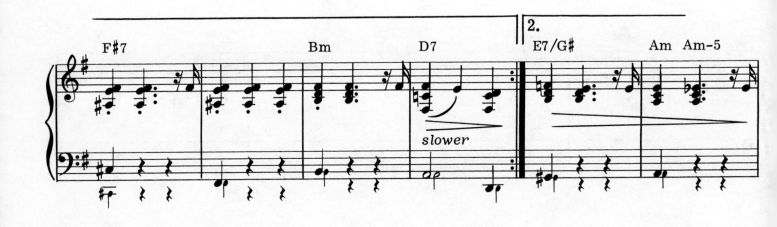

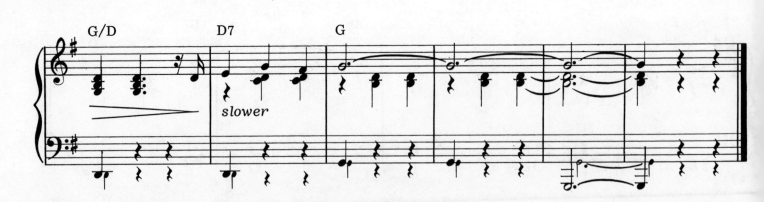

Gioacchino Rossini

WILLIAM TELL OVERTURE

Finale

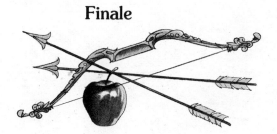

In 1829, at age 37, Rossini, who had already written 40 operas, was easily the most popular musician in the world. In Italy, his fellow countrymen affectionately referred to him as the Swan of Pesaro (his birthplace); in France, he was paid a pension that allowed him to feast on caviar, truffles and champagne every day. The Overture to *William Tell*, his last opera, is well known to every concert goer, and familiar to literally millions of people as the theme of *The Lone Ranger*. Simply hearing its opening fanfare (the first 12 bars below) makes one want to hop on a horse and join the chase.

Enrico Toselli

SERENADE

Toselli, handsome as a matinee idol and romantic as a prince in a fairy tale, wrote this "Serenade" just before his elopement with Princess Luisa of Saxony made him the talk—and the envy—of Europe in 1907. It was originally composed for a string quartet, but Toselli, himself a fine pianist, often performed alone what became his most popular melody. Shortly before Toselli died in 1926, his "Serenade" became the theme for the long-running radio and TV series *The Goldbergs*.

Sergei Prokofiev

MARCH

from
LOVE FOR THREE ORANGES

Russian composer Prokofiev was only 30 when he conducted the premiere of *Love for Three Oranges* in 1921. His opera concerns a storybook prince who ultimately discovers his fairy princess in the third of three oranges, whose love a wicked sorceress has doomed him to pursue. The "March" has long been a favorite with orchestras. It won a large new audience when it was used as a theme for the show *The FBI in Peace and War* on radio and TV, where its crackling energy and atmosphere of menace made it immediately recognizable.

Frédéric Chopin

ÉTUDE IN E
Opus 10, No. 3

(Transposed to G)

Chopin was only 21 when he arrived in Paris from Poland to seek his fortune. He immediately established his reputation by publishing his first 12 Études. These "studies" range from the violent "Revolutionary Étude" to this gentle, stately E major Étude, here transposed for easier playing to the key of G. Chopin's own playing is reported to have been very delicate and rather deliberate, two qualities of special importance for this piece.

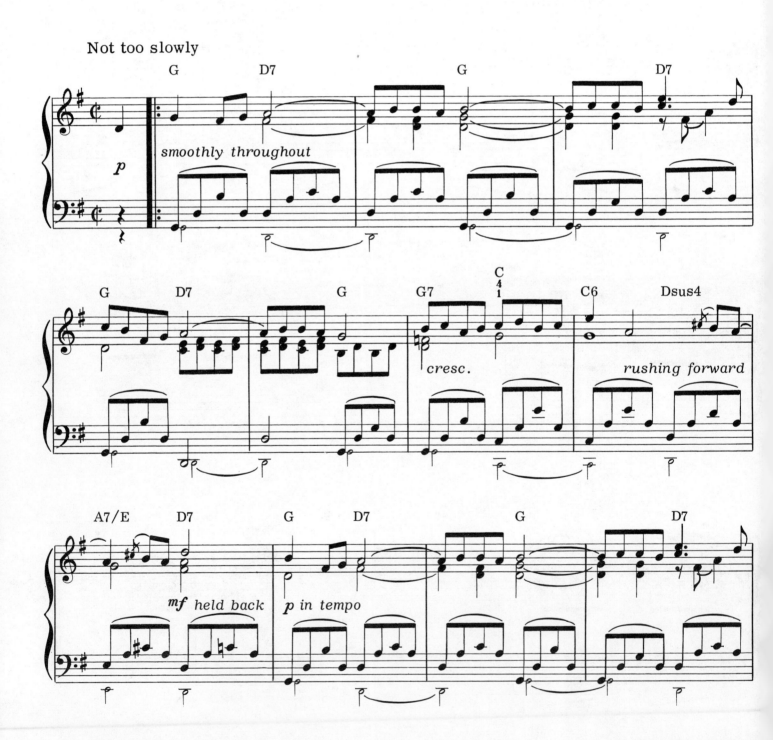

Not too slowly

smoothly throughout

cresc.

rushing forward

held back   in tempo

Georges Bizet

Farandole

from *L'ARLÉSIENNE*

In 1872 Bizet was asked to compose music for Alphonse Daudet's play *L'Arlésienne (The Woman from Arles)*. This was no small task in view of the fact that 27 musical pieces were needed, mostly as bridges between scenes; the time was short; and Bizet's state of health was precarious (in fact, he died just three years later, at the age of 36). For this "Farandole," Bizet used two 13th-century Provençal tunes—the first a sturdy march, and the second a skipping ditty which is the real farandole (an ancient fast dance done in a line with the dancers holding hands).

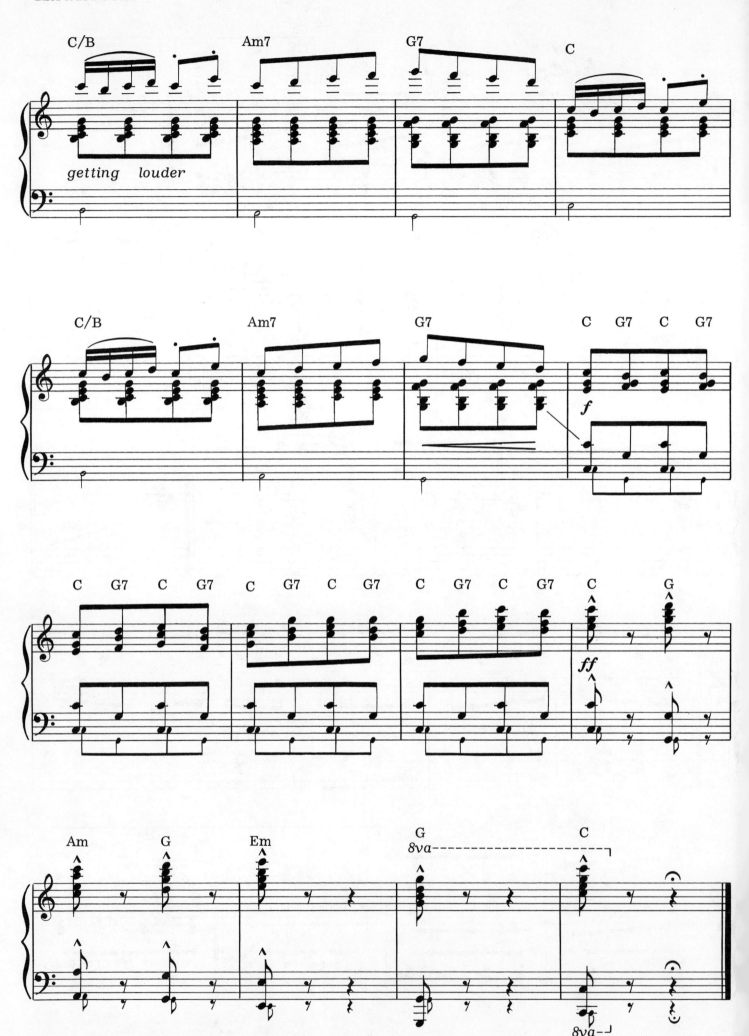

George Frederick Handel

LARGO

from the opera XERXES

As a musical term, "largo" means "very slow." And "Largo" has also become the name of Handel's most famous single melody, composed for his only comic opera, *Xerxes*, about the Persian king who found it easier to make war than love. The German-born Handel was revered in his adopted England, and the same year that saw the premiere in London of *Xerxes* —1738—also saw the erection of a life-size statue of its composer in that city's Vauxhall Gardens.

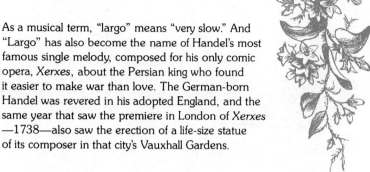

Slowly, with solemnity

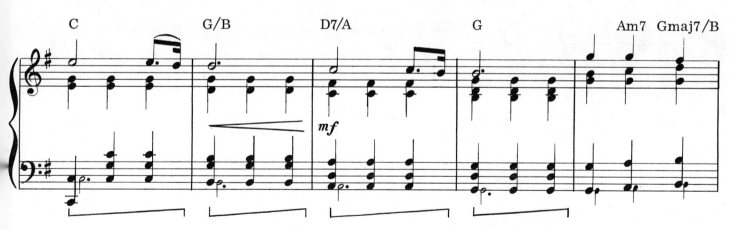

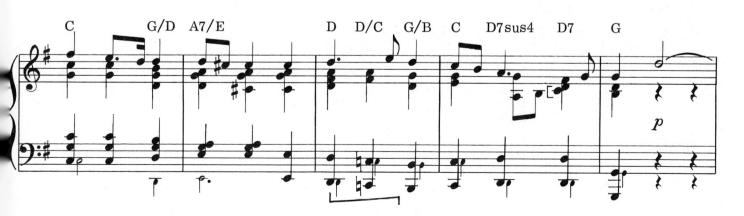

Handel: LARGO

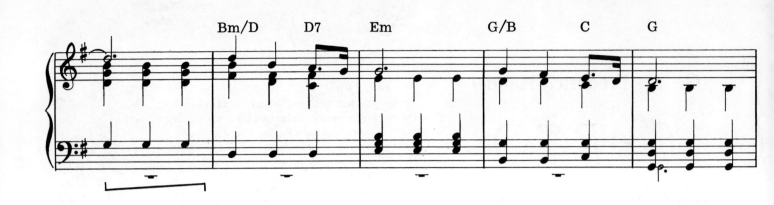

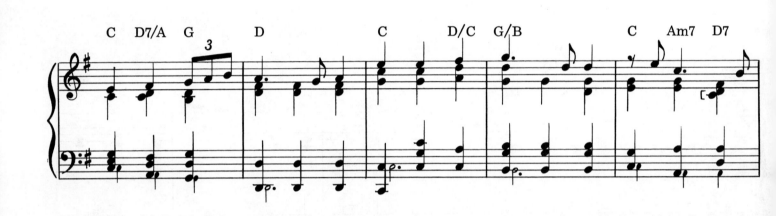

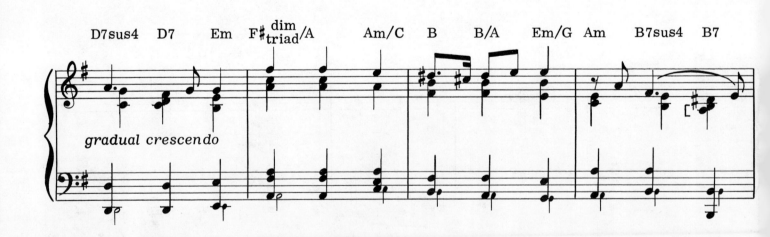

Hugo Alfvén

SWEDISH RHAPSODY
Opus 19

Alfvén, who was born in Stockholm in 1872, composed tunes so Swedish that they almost seem like folk music. Although he also wrote symphonies and other large-scale works, it is his "Swedish Rhapsody," with its polka-like rhythms and buoyant melodies, that has made Alfvén's name familiar throughout the world. First performed in the United States by the New York Symphony in 1922, soon after its composition, the "Swedish Rhapsody" has been a favorite of concert goers ever since.

Moderately fast

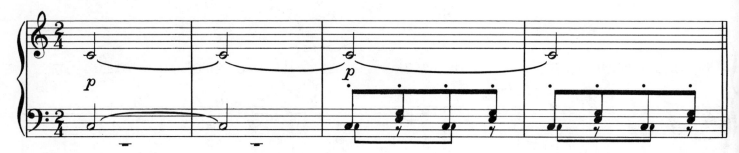

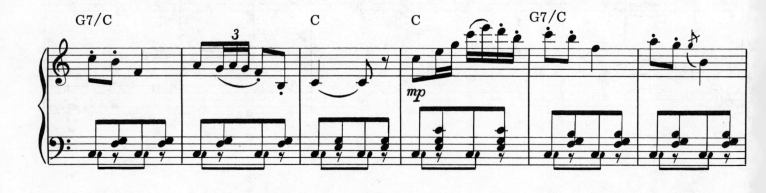

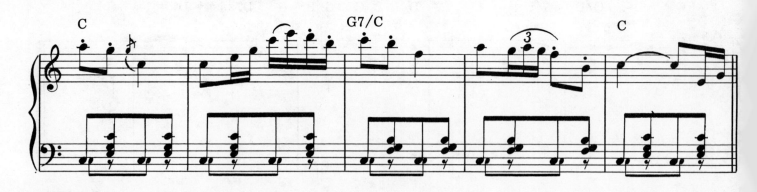

Nicolai Rimsky-Korsakov

SONG OF INDIA

from the opera SADKO

In Rimsky-Korsakov's opera *Sadko*, a homesick Hindu merchant, plying his wares in a gloomy Russian city, sings this song of his beloved India—of its warm sun, its sparkling rivers, its golden twilights. The melody of the Indian's song weaves up and down, suggesting all the color of his words, but you will notice that the entire harmony is based on a low G in the left hand which sounds throughout the piece. Tommy Dorsey and his orchestra made "Song of India" a swing hit in 1937.

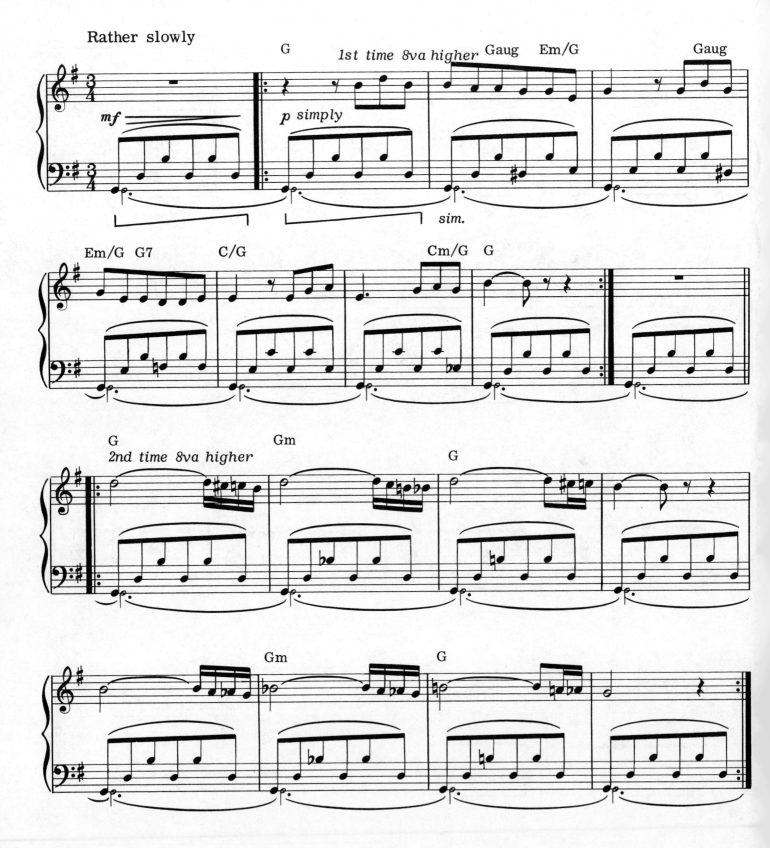

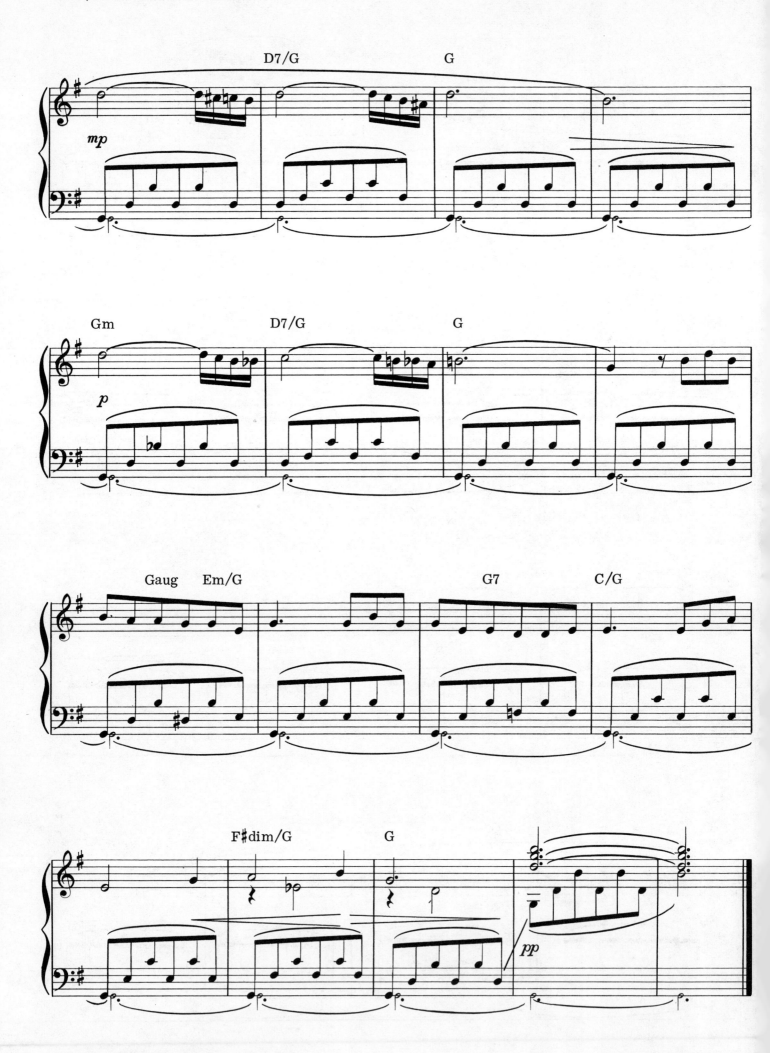

Peter Ilyich Tchaikovsky

The poem "None but the Lonely Heart" comes from Goethe's novel *Wilhelm Meisters Lehrjahre*, which Tchaikovsky read in the 1860s and immediately identified with, since, like Wilhelm, he was a young man, melancholy by nature and crossed in love. The composer had recently turned to songwriting, probably because of his friendship with the famous soprano Elizaveta Lavrovskaya. In 1869 he set Goethe's poem, which the heroine Mignon sings in the novel, to music (as did Ambroise Thomas in his opera *Mignon*, as "Connais-tu le pays?"), and its melody soon became one of his own favorites. Mlle. Lavrovskaya sang "None but the Lonely Heart" many times, but perhaps never to more acclaim than at a concert that the improvident composer gave in Moscow in 1871 to raise money for himself. The wide downward leaps of the song's vocal line are characteristic of Tchaikovsky, but their smoothness is difficult to duplicate on the piano.

Slowly, but not dragging

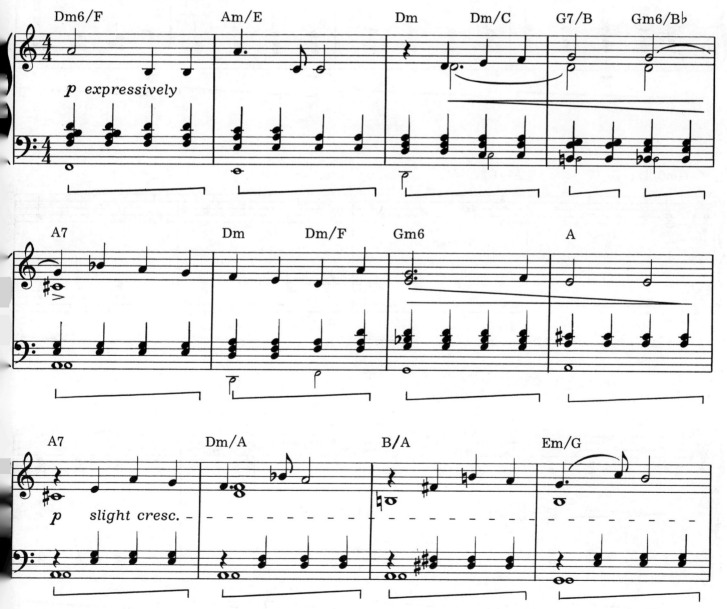

Antonín Dvořák

HUMORESQUE

Opus 101, No. 7

Dvořák's "Humoresque" appeared in print in the 1890s without fanfare, but became almost overnight one of the most famous melodies ever written. Dvořák, who traveled to the United States from his native Bohemia in 1892, professed that he found American music "magical" and "spacious." Little wonder, then, that some musical innovator later discovered that "Humoresque" could be sung or played simultaneously with Stephen Foster's "Way Down Upon the Swanee River." Try it!

Rather slowly and gracefully

Sergei Rachmaninoff

RHAPSODY ON A THEME BY PAGANINI
18th Variation

Niccolò Paganini (1782-1840), generally regarded as the greatest violin virtuoso of all time, published his Caprice No. 24 for solo violin in 1820, at the height of his fame in Paris. More than a century later, in 1934, Rachmaninoff composed his "Rhapsody on a Theme by Paganini," which takes the form of 24 variations on the violinist's Caprice. For the so-called "18th Variation," Rachmaninoff inverted the theme of the Caprice to achieve a magnificently romantic (and entirely new) melody. Just turn the music upside down, play the notes backward, and you will have Paganini's original motif.

Albert W. Ketelbey
IN A PERSIAN MARKET

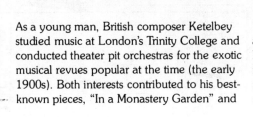

As a young man, British composer Ketelbey studied music at London's Trinity College and conducted theater pit orchestras for the exotic musical revues popular at the time (the early 1900s). Both interests contributed to his best-known pieces, "In a Monastery Garden" and "In a Persian Market"—two beautifully written and imaginatively scored musical fantasies. Notice the strong theme on page 105 entirely in fourths, for a mid-Eastern effect, and the meltingly romantic second theme which has made this piece a pops concert favorite.

104

*Optional: D.C. and fade

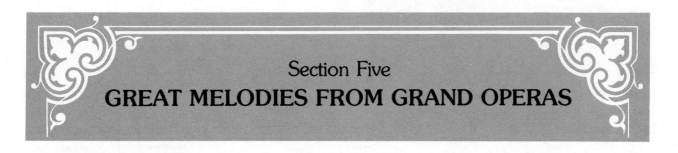

Jacques Offenbach

BARCAROLLE *from THE TALES OF HOFFMANN*

Offenbach made the German storywriter E.T.A. Hoffmann the hero of his last and greatest opera. The fantastic *Tales* that Hoffmann tells in the three-act opera concern three women whom he has loved passionately. One of the women, Giulietta, is an elegantly beautiful but unfeeling courtesan in the employ of a sinister magician. Giulietta tries to steal Hoffmann's soul by making him gaze into a mirror that is possessed of strange powers. Her seduction takes the form of a limpid barcarolle, or boat song, whose rhythm—a graceful, rocking 6/8—echoes the lapping waters of the Grand Canal in Venice, which her palace overlooks.

In a graceful 2 (♩. = 1 beat)

Giuseppe Verdi

La Donna È Mobile

from "Rigoletto"

In Verdi's *Rigoletto*, the Duke of Mantua, a handsome, licentious nobleman, seduces every pretty girl he meets. Before pursuing his next innocent prey, he excuses his deed by singing "La Donna È Mobile" (Woman Is Fickle). In the opera (based on a play by Victor Hugo and first performed in Venice in 1851), this prancing melody is sung twice; repeat the entire arrangement, including the introductory two lines, for the effect closest to the operatic original.

Moderately, with spirit

110

Georges Bizet

TOREADOR SONG

from CARMEN

Just as in the "Habanera" (see page 115) Carmen boasts about her knowledge of love and her proficiency in it, so in the "Toreador Song" the bullfighter Escamillo boasts about his profession. The song, which is from the second act of Bizet's opera *Carmen*, is divided into a dramatic martial section in which Escamillo sings of the dangers of bullfighting, and a somewhat more expansive section (the famous "Toreador" refrain) in which he describes the pleasures and honors of the ring.

Georges Bizet

HABANERA
from CARMEN

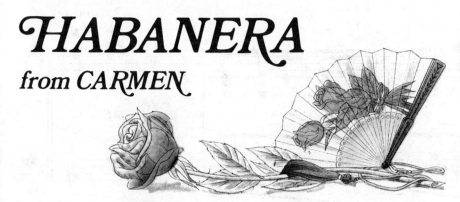

Bizet's famous opera *Carmen* is about a sultry young flirt who works in a cigarette factory in Seville, Spain. At the beginning of the opera, as the workers loll about the town square on their midday break, Carmen sings the "Habanera," in which she boasts that she knows all there is to know about love. The gypsy's song attracts the attention of Don José, an army corporal, who, as the opera progresses, arrests her for stabbing a fellow worker, then helps her escape, falls in love with her, and eventually kills her when she tires of him. The audience at the Paris premiere of *Carmen* in 1875 found the story a bit extreme for its taste, and the opera did not attain popularity until it was performed in Vienna four months later.

Allegretto (not fast)

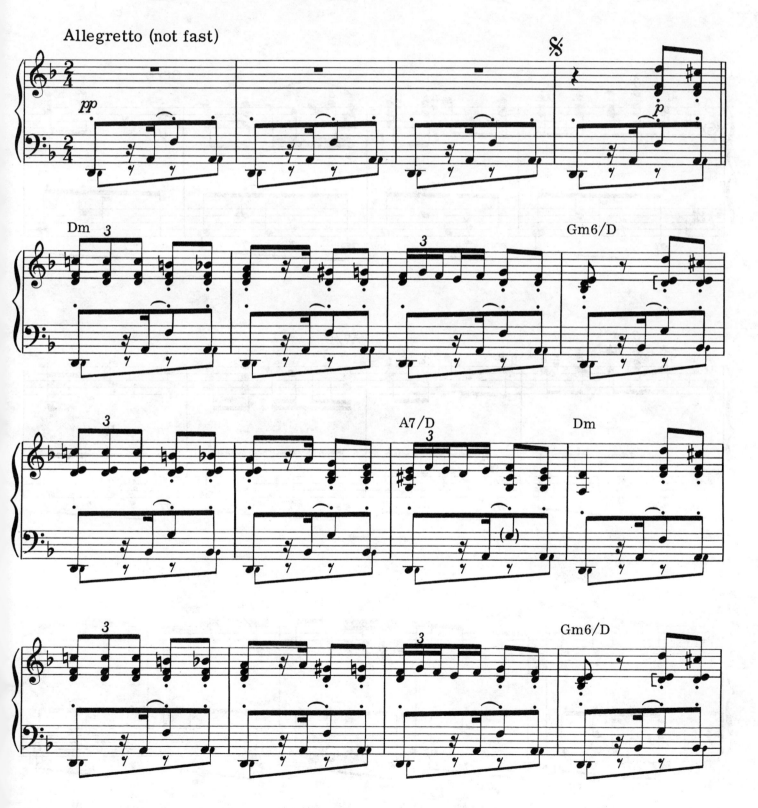

Pietro Mascagni

INTERMEZZO *from CAVALLERIA RUSTICANA*

Mascagni's one-act opera *Cavalleria Rusticana*, which, in 1890, opened the door to naturalism in opera, tells the story of a tragic love triangle. Those involved are Turiddu, a carefree young Sicilian soldier; Santuzza, the woman whom he seduces and abandons; and Lola, the faithless wife of a fellow townsman. The time is Easter Sunday. By the hour for Mass, Santuzza has abased herself with her frantic pleading for love, and Lola has openly flirted with Turiddu, who, in turn, has cruelly repulsed Santuzza and encouraged Lola. When the bells ring for Mass, the stage empties, and this "Intermezzo," with its magnificent serenity, is heard, played by the orchestra. The piece begins pianissimo, rises to a sonorous climax, and then subsides in an eddy of golden light—the last six measures of this arrangement, which rise in soft arpeggios like incense from the altar of the village church.

Giacomo Puccini

Musetta's Waltz

from "La Bohème"

The second act of Puccini's *La Bohème* takes place on Christmas Eve in the Café Momus in the Latin Quarter of Paris. In her famous waltz, Musetta, once the darling of the painter Marcello and now the companion of the wealthy old man Alcindoro, seeks to attract the eye of her former lover, and succeeds admirably. She sings her gay song, dances, wheedles Marcello into romantic humor, and then goes off with him, leaving the befuddled Alcindoro to pay the bill.

Freely and rapidly

Slow waltz

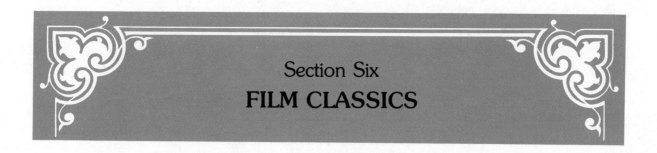

Section Six
FILM CLASSICS

Charles Williams
Theme from "The Apartment"

In creating his musical score for the 1960 film *The Apartment*, Adolph Deutsch incorporated a song that had been written by someone else, in 1949. The composer was Charles Williams, an Englishman, and the song was "Jealous Lover." Used as the theme music of the film, which starred Shirley MacLaine and Jack Lemmon, it was played by a solo piano, with haunting effect. The arpeggiated chords indicated in our arrangement for the left hand crossed over the right (as in line 2, measure 2) may be played with the right hand, if easier.

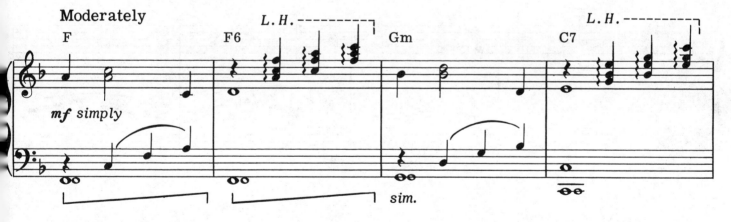

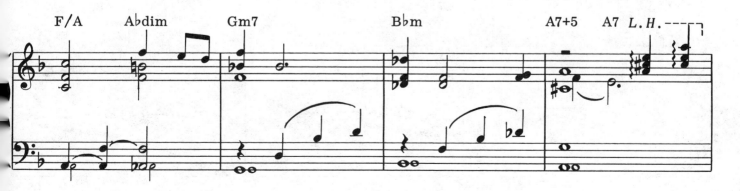

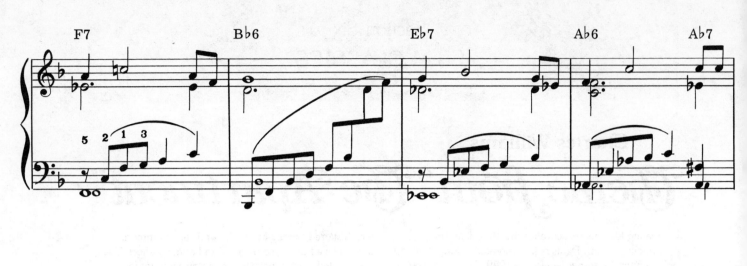

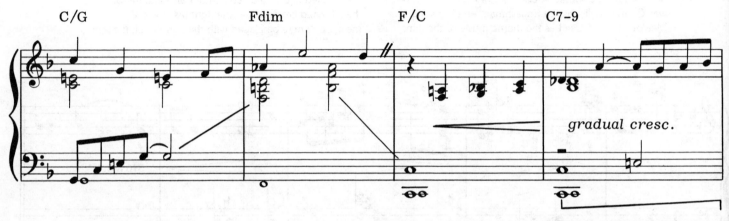

Broadly

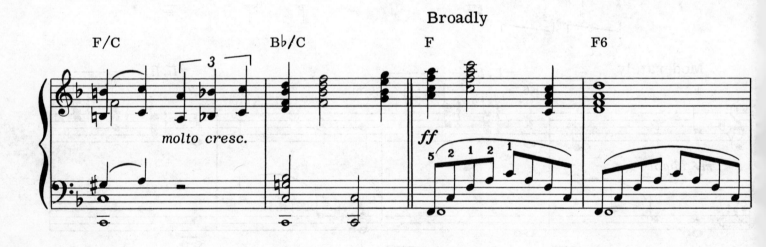

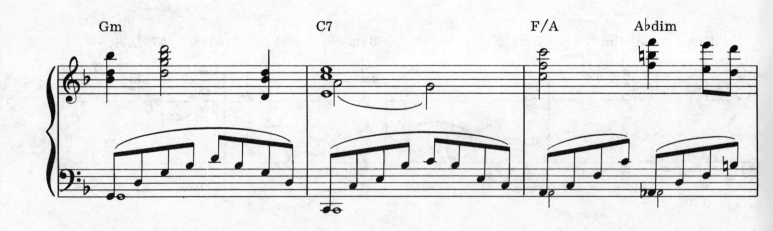

Johannes Brahms

SYMPHONY No. 3

Third Movement Theme

The 1947 film *Song of Love* told the story of the compulsively passionate composer-critic Robert Schumann; his wife Clara—a strong-minded pianist who lived in an era in which most professional musicians were men; and Johannes Brahms, the young composer whose genius the Schumanns recognized and encouraged. The movie's brooding musical theme was taken from Brahms' Third Symphony, which was in fact written in 1883, 27 years after Schumann had died in an insane asylum.

Not too slow

Richard Addinsell

Warsaw Concerto

from SUICIDE SQUADRON

English composer Addinsell wrote the "Warsaw Concerto" for a British World War II film, released in this country in 1942 as *Suicide Squadron*. The concerto bristles with pyrotechnical solo passages for the piano, but it was the gleaming melody of the songful second section that made Addinsell's reputation enviable. The right-hand glissando which adds so much to the brilliant ending should be played with the backs of two fingers; the left-hand glissando, with the back of the thumb.

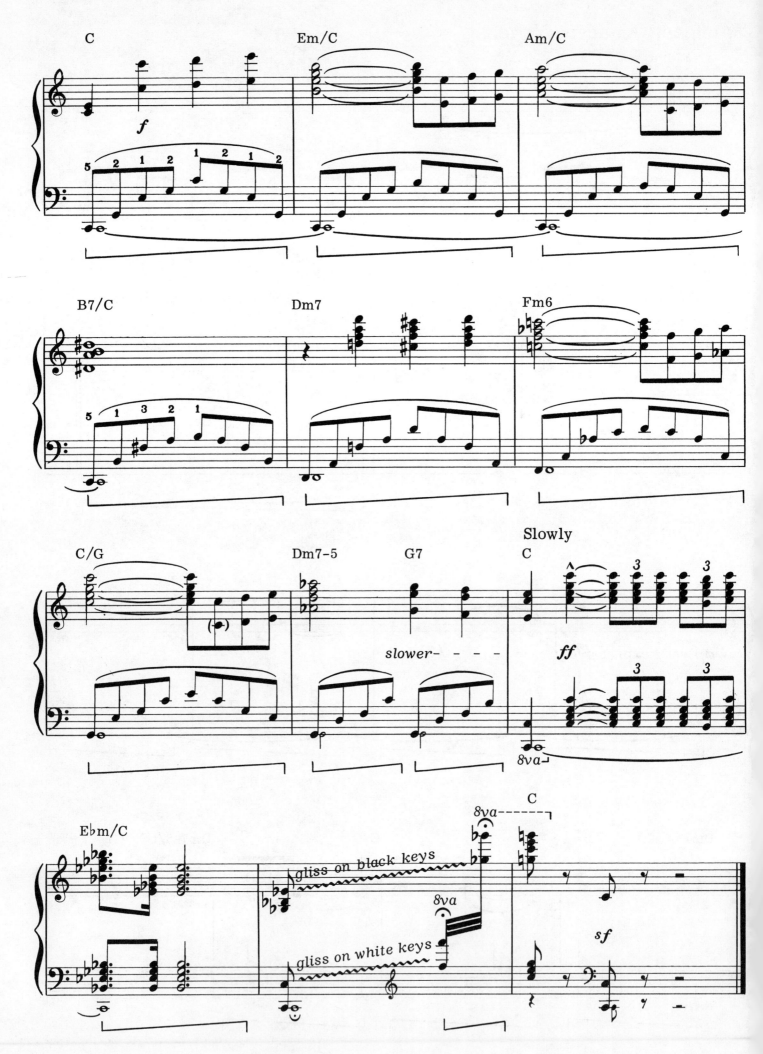

Wolfgang Amadeus Mozart

Andante

from
Concerto No. 21 in C Major

Mozart was happily married and living in Vienna when he wrote his Piano Concerto in C Major in 1785. Haydn, then the reigning king of music, called him "the greatest composer known to me." In short, Mozart was a happy man and a successful musician—and the beauty of this slow movement theme reflects his contentment. Always much admired, it attained new popularity when it was used in the 1967 Swedish film of two doomed lovers, *Elvira Madigan*.

Andante (flowing along; not fast)

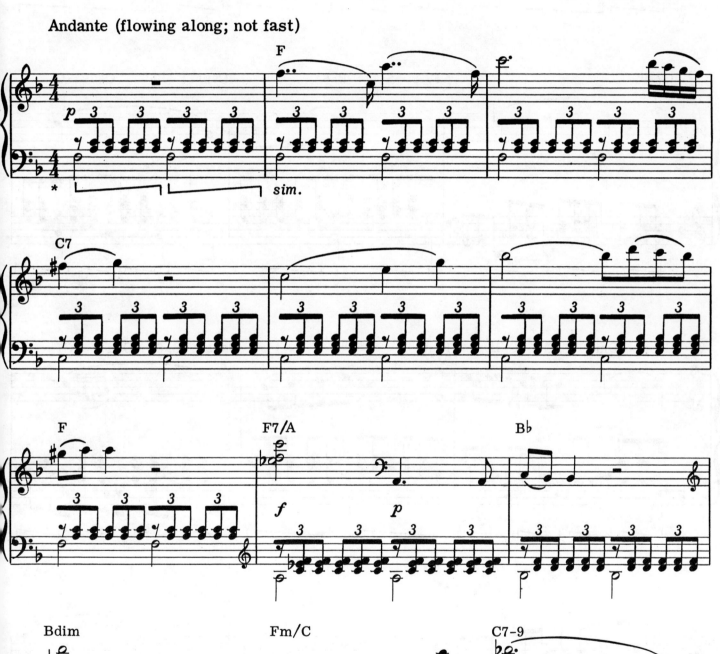

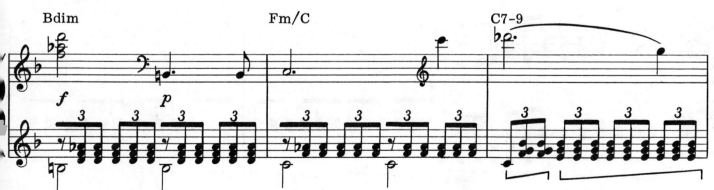

Although not indicated, organ pedal may double piano left hand an 8va lower throughout.

131

Richard Strauss

ALSO SPRACH ZARATHUSTRA

(Portion used in the film 2001: A SPACE ODYSSEY)

Stanley Kubrick's 1968 science-fiction film *2001: A Space Odyssey* opened with one of filmdom's most arresting scenes. The impact was both visual—a planet slowly rising in outer space—and aural— the opening measures of this tone poem by Richard Strauss. The music, based on the work by the philosopher Nietzsche, dates from 1896, but sounds uncannily contemporary. The piece begins with a pianissimo low C and rises to a climax which is shattering in its simplicity.

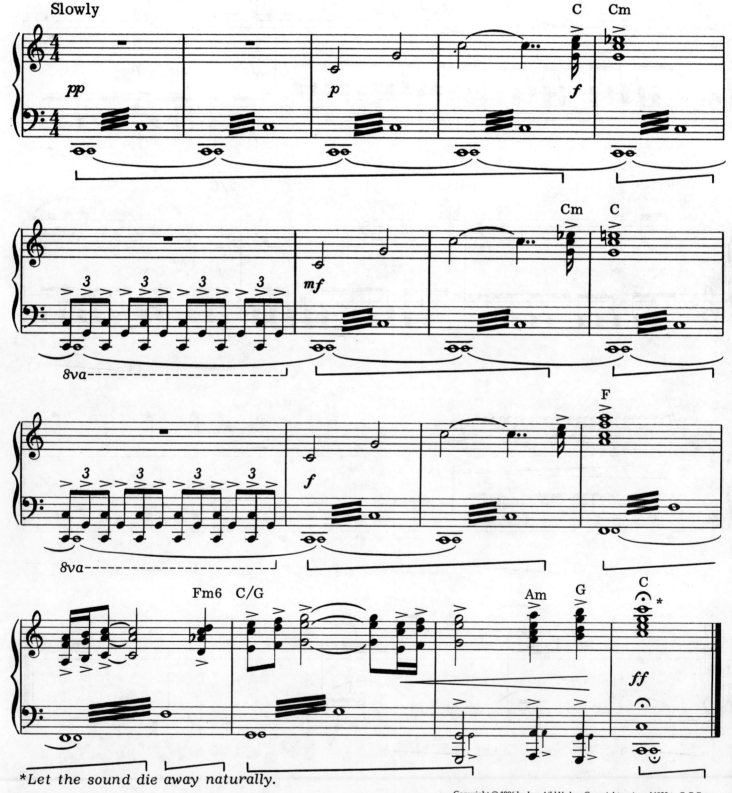

Let the sound die away naturally.

Heinz Provost

INTERMEZZO

Theme from
INTERMEZZO —A LOVE STORY

The 1939 film *Intermezzo* introduced the radiant Swedish star Ingrid Bergman to American moviegoers. In it she played a pianist who falls in love with a married violinist (Leslie Howard)—an accurate bit of casting since she had trained to become a concert pianist before taking up acting. This lovely theme served as a kind of courtship ritual with its mixture of romance and pathos. The clusters of sixteenth notes (as in the third complete measure) may be more comfortably played by taking the first four notes with the right hand, the second four with the left, and, in this case, the final note with the right.

135

George Frederick Handel
SARABANDE from Suite No. 11

In addition to composing choral and orchestral works, Handel also wrote suites—mostly dances and other short sketches—for the harpsichord which were wildly popular among amateur players of the period. This stately dance from his Suite No. 11 and two variations on it (one of which is included in our arrangement) were issued in 1733 by Handel's publisher, who neglected even to obtain the composer's permission to print his work. The Sarabande reached a host of new admirers as the theme of Stanley Kubrick's 1975 film version of Thackeray's novel *Barry Lyndon*.

Richard Rodgers

The Carousel Waltz from CAROUSEL

"The most glorious of the Rodgers and Hammerstein works," acclaimed New York *Times* critic Brooks Atkinson of *Carousel* when it returned to Broadway in 1954, nine years after its first triumphant appearance. The saga of a New England circus barker and the girl he loves, the musical is studded with R&H classics—"If I Loved You," "June

Is Bustin' Out All Over," "You'll Never Walk Alone"—and Rodgers' solo effort, "The Carousel Waltz." The waltz opens the show and immediately transports us to the whirling, joyous world of the small-town amusement park in which the story is set. Later, as Billy disconsolately wanders the park, the waltz is heard again, in a minor key.

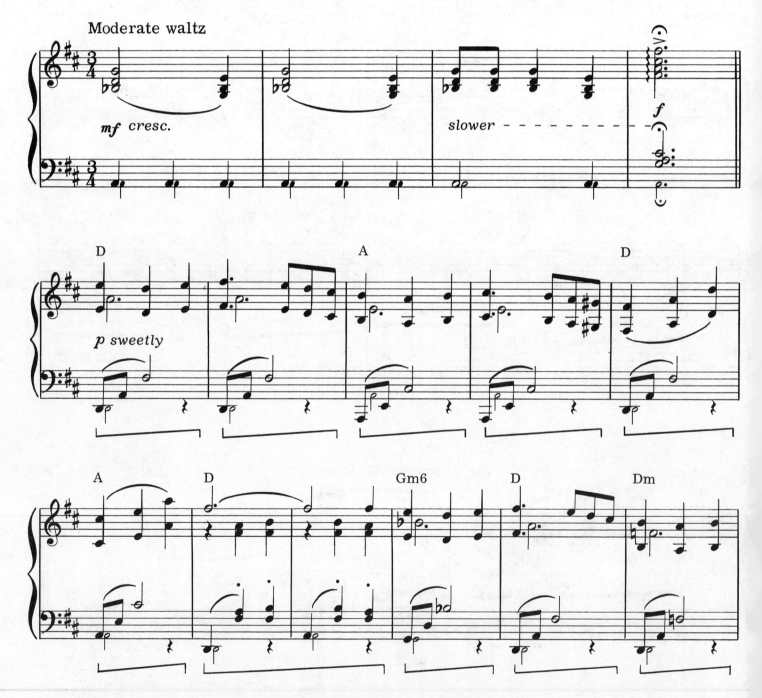

Richard Rodgers
The March of the Siamese Children
from THE KING AND I

Richard Rodgers said that, before composing the score for *The King and I,* he "couldn't have written an authentic Far Eastern melody if my life depended on it." But then he wrote "The March of the Siamese Children," and fooled everyone. The quaint effect of the B natural in the first phrase and the downward fifths in the second section produce a marvelously Oriental effect, which made the "March" a highlight of the 1951 musical.

Alexander Borodin

POLOVETSIAN DANCE №. 2

from PRINCE IGOR

In Borodin's lushly scored opera *Prince Igor,* the Prince leaves Moscow to wage a military campaign against the nomadic Polovetskis in eastern Russia, and is taken prisoner by them. In the Polovetski camp Igor watches the young warriors dance—the most incredibly athletic leaps and turns in a turmoil of competitive display. But the dancers have their more lyric, graceful moments, too. For their 1953 musical *Kismet,* George Forrest and Robert Wright selected the lovely Polovetsian Dance No. 2 as the basis for "Stranger in Paradise," a duet between the poet's daughter and the young caliph who has fallen in love with her.

In a moderate 2 (♩=1 beat)

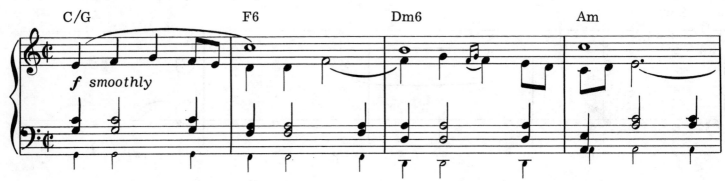

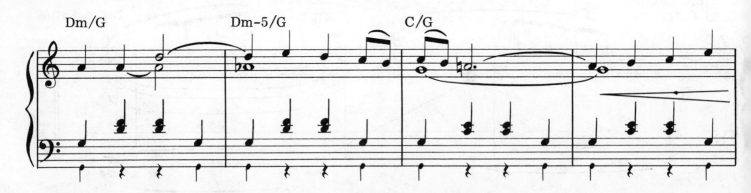

Alexander Borodin

NOCTURNE
from String Quartet No. 2 in D

"A musical Arabian Night"—that's how George Forrest and Robert Wright described their 1953 Broadway hit *Kismet*, which they based on the music of Russian composer Alexander Borodin. The languorous melody of the slow movement from Borodin's Second String Quartet, which furnished the music for *Kismet*'s "And This Is My Beloved," fitted perfectly into the exotic setting of the show, which won a Tony award for best musical in 1954. Borodin completed his Quartet in 1887.

Not too slow

Edvard Grieg

PIANO CONCERTO
Opus 16

First Movement, Main Theme

Grieg was only 25 when he composed his Piano Concerto in 1868. But the work was so typically Scandinavian in melody and so pianistic in style that it earned the Norwegian composer the nickname "Chopin of the North." When George Forrest and Robert Wright wrote their successful 1944 Broadway musical *Song of Norway*, based on Grieg's music, they made the opening theme of the Concerto, with its crash of downward chords, one of their main melodies.

150

Franz Schubert

SYMPHONY No. 8 IN B MINOR

("The Unfinished")

First Movement Theme

When Schubert died at 31, he left us his imperishable symphonies. His life, itself a pathetic symphony of non-recognition, poverty and illness, was glamorized in *Blossom Time,* a 1921 musical for which Sigmund Romberg adapted Schubert's melodies. For "Song of Love," the show's big hit, Romberg used the first movement theme of the "Unfinished" Symphony, so-called because the third and fourth movements were either lost or never written.

Victor Herbert

MARCH OF THE TOYS
from BABES IN TOYLAND

Inspired by the success of Frank Baum's *Wizard of Oz* books, Victor Herbert in 1903 created a Broadway equivalent with a fairy-tale background. *Babes in Toyland,* for all its childlike simplicity, set the Great White Way on its ear. "Ingenious and brilliant, with rich and dazzling costumes, and music a hundred times better than the usual," wrote one critic. The "March of the Toys," performed for the operetta's runaway children, Jane and Alan, combines a perky rhythm with an amusingly grotesque melody.

Moderate march tempo

(No chords)

Herbert: MARCH OF THE TOYS

156

Section Eight
REVERIES, NOCTURNES AND SERENADES

Frédéric Chopin

NOCTURNE IN E FLAT, Opus 9, No. 2
(Transposed to C)

Chopin's familiar Nocturne in E Flat (here transposed to the easier key of C major) was among the first of the many nocturnes that he published. It appeared in 1833, when the 23-year-old composer had just become the toast of Paris, and was a piano teacher in great social demand among the wealthy. "Carriages and white gloves cost a pretty penny," he wrote to a friend, "and without them one would not be in good taste." Fortunately he was, in his own words, "making a fortune." Chopin dedicated the nocturne to one of the most prominent and beautiful women in Paris, Mme. Camille Pleyel, wife of a leading piano manufacturer and herself a charming player. She was among those who welcomed the young Pole when, at the age of 21, he arrived in the French capital half dead of exhaustion from his trip from Warsaw. This nocturne (or "night piece") was the basis of "My Twilight Dream," the theme song of Eddy Duchin, a popular pianist-bandleader of the 1930s and early '40s.

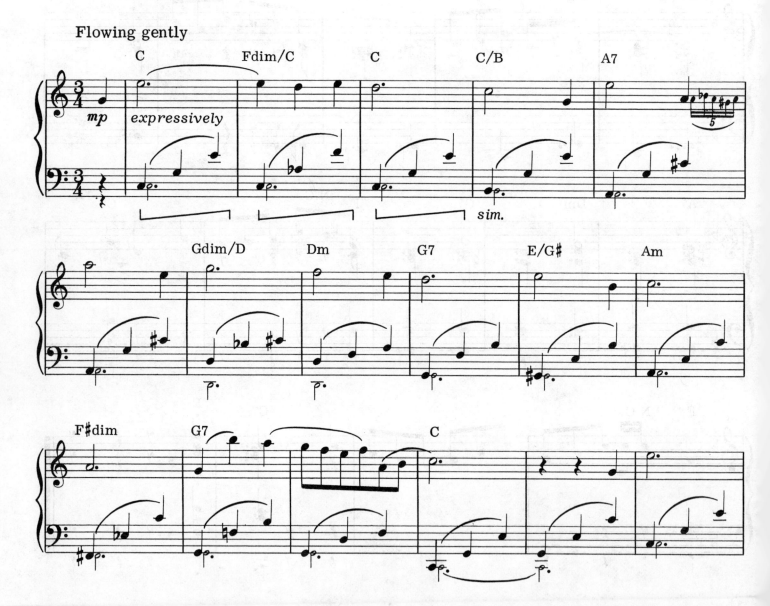

Peter Ilyich Tchaikovsky

Waltz *from "Serenade for Strings"*

Tchaikovsky had one of his greatest successes with this lovely waltz from the "Serenade for Strings." He wrote the "Serenade" in 1880, and it must have been a great relief from the spirited "1812 Overture" which he was composing at the same time. Of the "Serenade," Tchaikovsky said,

"It is a piece from the heart; I can't wait for it to be played." He himself conducted several of its early performances. However, the composer had had no formal training with the baton and suffered so much from stage fright that he occasionally lost the place even in his own music.

Moderately

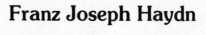

Franz Joseph Haydn

SERENADE
from String Quartet in F, Opus 3, No. 5

Familiarly known as "Haydn's Serenade," this work is actually the slow movement from one of the composer's string quartets, written around 1772. Haydn spent 30 of his most musically productive years in the service of a wealthy and aristocratic Hungarian family, the Esterházys, who not only maintained a magnificent palace in Eisenstadt, south of Vienna, but kept a string quartet and an entire opera company in residence. The original of the "Serenade" has the first violin playing legato and the other three instruments pizzicato, an effect that can be approximated by playing the left hand staccato and very light.

During his tragically short life of 31 years, Schubert composed more than 600 songs, a melodic outpouring that, to date, has never been equaled in quantity or quality. The first songs he wrote date from 1811, when he was 14; the last, from the year he died. "Serenade," a particular favorite, is one of the latter songs, which was set to a poem by Ludwig Rellstab, and was not published until after Schubert's death in 1828, as part of the collection of songs called "Schwanengesang." With the harmonizing of the melody in sixths (on page 167) or thirds, and with the accompaniment mostly of simple chords played staccato, this song resembles a Venetian serenade, to be sung with the singer's own guitar echoing the lapping of the water in the canals.

Franz Schubert

Serenade

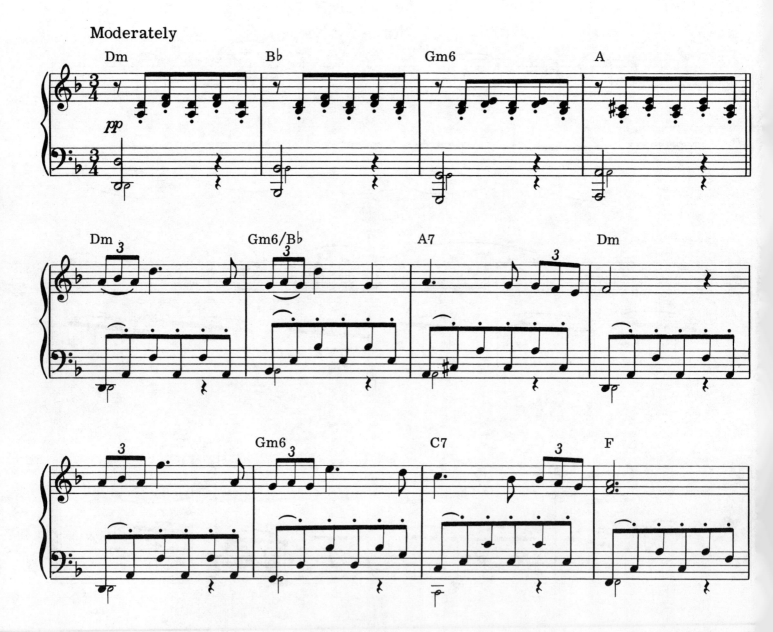

Robert Schumann

TRÄUMEREI

No. 7 from KINDERSCENEN

Schumann composed "Träumerei," one of the 13 pieces in his collection of *Scenes from Childhood*, in 1838, shortly after he became engaged to Clara Wieck. He wrote to his fiancée that the selections were peaceful, tender and happy—"like our future." You will discover in playing the song that in the first full chord the left and right hands overlap. This is a curiosity of Schumann's own scoring, but the notes can be easily rearranged for a simpler execution if desired.

Moderately and somewhat freely

Riccardo Drigo

SERENADE

from the ballet
HARLEQUIN'S MILLIONS

Though Drigo was born and educated in Padua, and eventually died there in 1930 at the age of 84, he spent most of his life among Russian royalty in St. Petersburg, as conductor of the Marinsky Theater. His years in St. Petersburg—from 1878 to 1915—were fascinating ones; he witnessed, for example, the premieres of Tchaikovsky's last ballets, even contributing some music to them. His own ballet *Harlequin's Millions* was first danced there, its score highlighted by the famous "Serenade." The ballet's story concerns a poor but amorous youth named Harlequin whose efforts to win the affection of Columbine are frustrated by her rich and stingy father, Cassandre, who intends to auction her off, and even has a wealthy old reprobate hanging on his coattails panting to make a bid. Cassandre is exasperated by Harlequin's poverty and by his attempts to court Columbine surreptitiously. But the Good Fairy, who apparently cannot resist the "Serenade" any more than Columbine can, comes to the aid of the lovers and magically causes whole cornucopias of gold to materialize from nowhere. Cassandre is satisfied; the ancient suitor is sent packing; and Harlequin and Columbine are finally united forever.

Andante cantabile

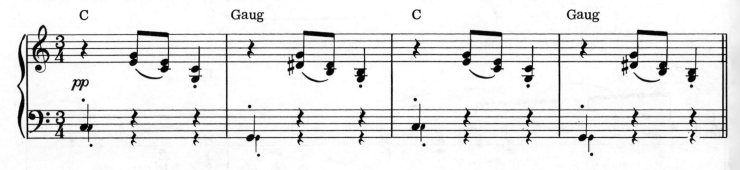

A little more sustained

2nd time, 8va higher; Mandolin imitation ad lib.

Franz Liszt

LIEBESTRAUM

(Dream of Love)

Franz Liszt, wildly handsome and hugely talented, cut a wide swath in Paris in the 1830s, where it is said that women actually swooned at his piano recitals. In 1850, living more quietly in Weimar, Liszt transcribed three of his own songs for piano, calling them "Liebesträume," or "Dreams of Love." The first and most popular one is a romantic symbol nonpareil. In this arrangement of it, the original scoring for crossed hands has been incorporated, beginning with the 11th measure on page 174. If too difficult, the measures marked 1 to 2 may be substituted for those marked 3 to 4.

Very slowly, in 2 (each ♩. = 1 beat)

with a singing tone

sim.

getting slightly louder and more agitated

Liszt: LIEBESTRAUM

174

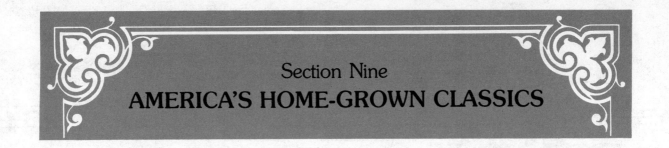

Section Nine
AMERICA'S HOME-GROWN CLASSICS

Edward MacDowell

To a Wild Rose
from "Woodland Sketches"

Woodland Sketches (1896) is one of the works that established MacDowell as the first internationally recognized American composer of genius. "To a Wild Rose," the opening piece, is his best-known and best-loved song. In addition to such exquisite miniatures, he also composed symphonic poems, orchestral suites, piano sonatas, and concertos for piano and orchestra, and, from 1896 to 1904, headed the newly formed department of music at Columbia University in New York. He and his wife spent their summers at the New Hampshire artist colony which today bears his name.

With simple tenderness

176

(Bring out this line)

Scott Joplin
MAPLE LEAF RAG

In the 1890s, Scott Joplin was playing ragtime as the resident pianist of the Maple Leaf Club in Sedalia, Missouri. He took one of his own rags, called "The Maple Leaf," to John Stark, a music store owner and publisher. Stark bought the piece, published it, and got rich. Joplin didn't get rich from "Maple Leaf Rag," but the resultant publicity and the subsequent rags he wrote earned him the title King of Ragtime. Eventually his music sold so well that he was able to afford a huge house in St. Louis—rather unusual for a black musician in those days—and an ebony grand piano as long as a caboose.

Scott Joplin

Although "Solace" is not one of Joplin's typical rags, it does have rhythmic elements of his inimitable style, even if its mood on the whole is more sedate than that of his other published rags. After many years of wandering from place to place, and playing one-night stands in wicked cities like New Orleans and Chicago, Joplin settled in Missouri. There he wrote "Solace" and other rags, and began work on an opera, *Treemonisha*, which was not produced until 1975, 58 years after the composer's death. "Solace" is one of the Joplin tunes that spiced the 1973 film *The Sting*.

Very slow march time, in 2 (♩=1 beat)

Leroy Anderson
FORGOTTEN DREAMS

As with so many other tunes by Leroy Anderson, this one was first performed and recorded by the Boston Pops Orchestra under the direction of Arthur Fiedler, for whom Anderson served at one time as arranger and assistant conductor. Most of the piece was scored for the string instruments of the orchestra, so the more smoothly and shimmeringly the parts can be played on the piano (we suggest that you pedal with each change of left-hand harmony), the better.

Delicately, not too fast

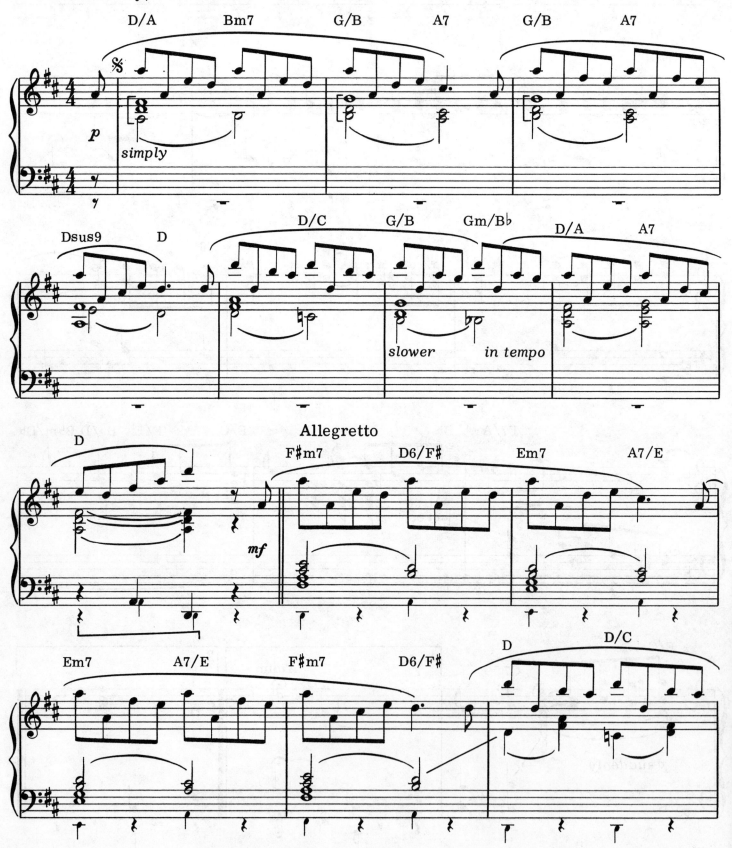

George Gershwin

Rhapsody in Blue

Getting his first job in Tin Pan Alley at 16, Brooklyn-born George Gershwin plugged other people's songs until he discovered that he could write better ones himself. His first musical, *La, La, Lucille*, produced on Broadway in 1919, when he was 21, and subsequent ones earned him such fame that just five years later bandleader Paul Whiteman asked him to write a piece for his "Experiment in Modern Music" concert at New York's prestigious Aeolian Hall. "Rhapsody in Blue" was the result. Not only did it "make a lady out of jazz," but it also established Gershwin as America's most exciting composer. It took him only 10 days to write the music, and he himself played the piano solo at the premiere. The long trill and upward run is one of the most famous beginnings in all music, and, played by a wailing clarinet, sounded to one critic like a chuckle turning into a laugh.

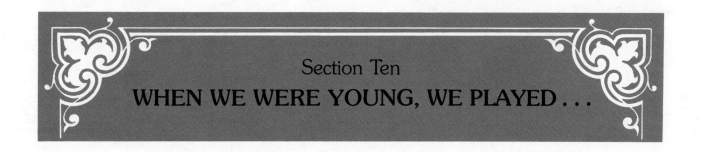

Section Ten
WHEN WE WERE YOUNG, WE PLAYED . . .

Ludwig van Beethoven

FÜR ELISE

When Beethoven composed this piece around 1810, he described it as a little "bagatelle" and hastily scribbled a title on it, which we know as "Für Elise." Now, however, music scholars believe that Beethoven's illegible title was really "Für Therese," and the composition intended as a gift for Therese Malfatti, his physician's daughter. The rather melancholy air of the piece is heightened on page 191, where the repeated single notes in the left hand are easiest played by using the same finger, say the third, rather than trying to alternate two or more fingers.

Slowly, in 1 (each measure = 1 beat)

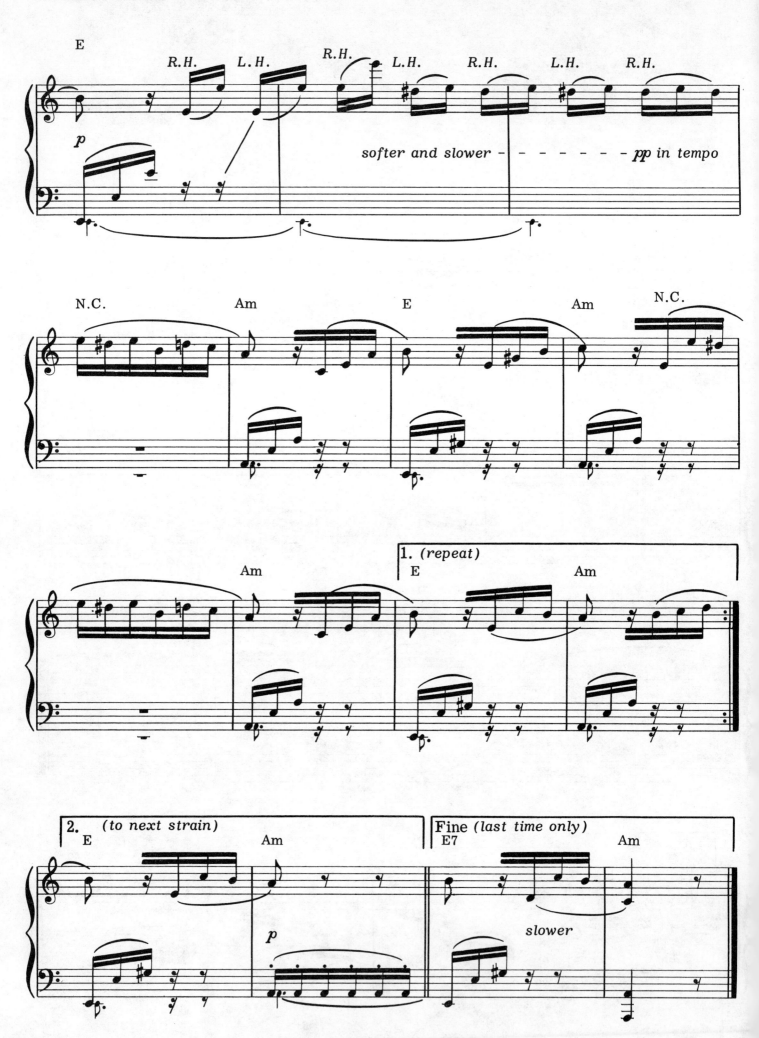

Ludwig van Beethoven
MINUET IN G

Beethoven was only one of many composers who used the appealing 3/4 rhythm of the minuet in writing little teaching pieces for the piano. His Minuet in G, perhaps the most famous ever written, was published as one of a half-dozen dances composed, we presume, for the children of some wealthy patron. The piece should not be played too fast, nor should the second section be speeded up. Custom also dictates that when the first page is played for the second time, after the Trio, the repeats are not taken.

Johann Sebastian Bach

BOURRÉE

from The Anna Magdalena Notebook

Like the Minuet (also from *The Anna Magdalena Notebook*) on page 8 of this book, this bourrée by Bach is composed of a single line of notes for each hand. The bourrée was a dance that originated in 17th-century Auvergne, one of the mountainous provinces in central France. It was first described in a musical dictionary dated 1615, and was later included in groups of dances that were composed

and published as suites. Bach wrote much of his finest keyboard music in the early 1720s, due to the fact that the royal employer for whom he worked was a Calvinist whose austere religious services offered Bach little or no opportunity to compose church music. However, his prowess on all keyboard instruments—harpsichord, clavichord, organ—served him well in technical studies.

For hints on performance, see TWO-PART INVENTION on page 196.

Johann Sebastian Bach

Two-part Invention No.1 in C

Bach, who wrote some of his finest music as teaching material, composed the 15 Inventions in 1720 for his own children. They were never published during his lifetime, and perhaps never performed by anyone outside his family. An invention is a piece for two "voices," one played entirely by the right hand, the other by the left, and the two imitate each other's melodies and rhythms. The piece is challenging to play because the left hand is expected to be as fully independent as the right.

Some performance notes:

The abbreviation ⏦ (called a short trill) means to play the note above the written note, then the written note, the note above and finally the written note. Thus is played.

The abbreviation ⏦ (called an inverted mordent) means to play the written note, the note below it, then the written note. Thus is played.

The chord symbols in parentheses are only approximations. The great J.S. Bach wrote in a contrapuntal style which created chords very rapidly one after the other. The notated chords reflect only the general impression of the harmony created by the counterpoint.

Moderately fast

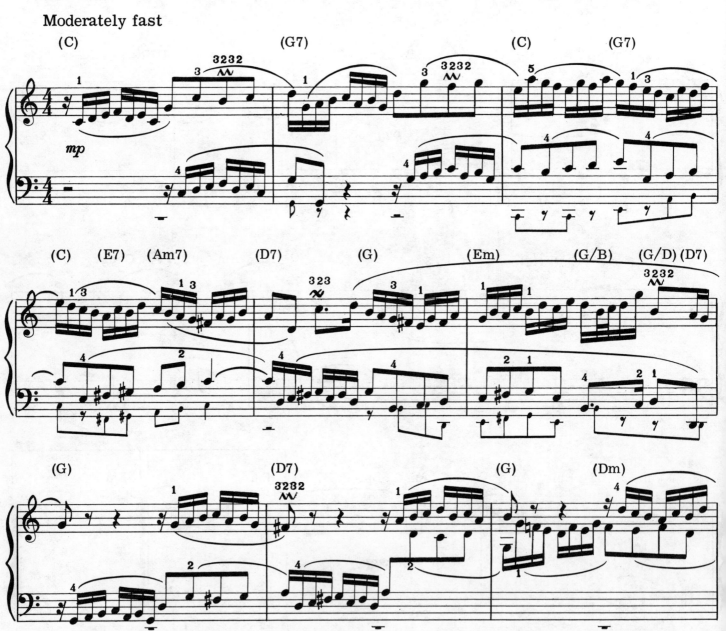

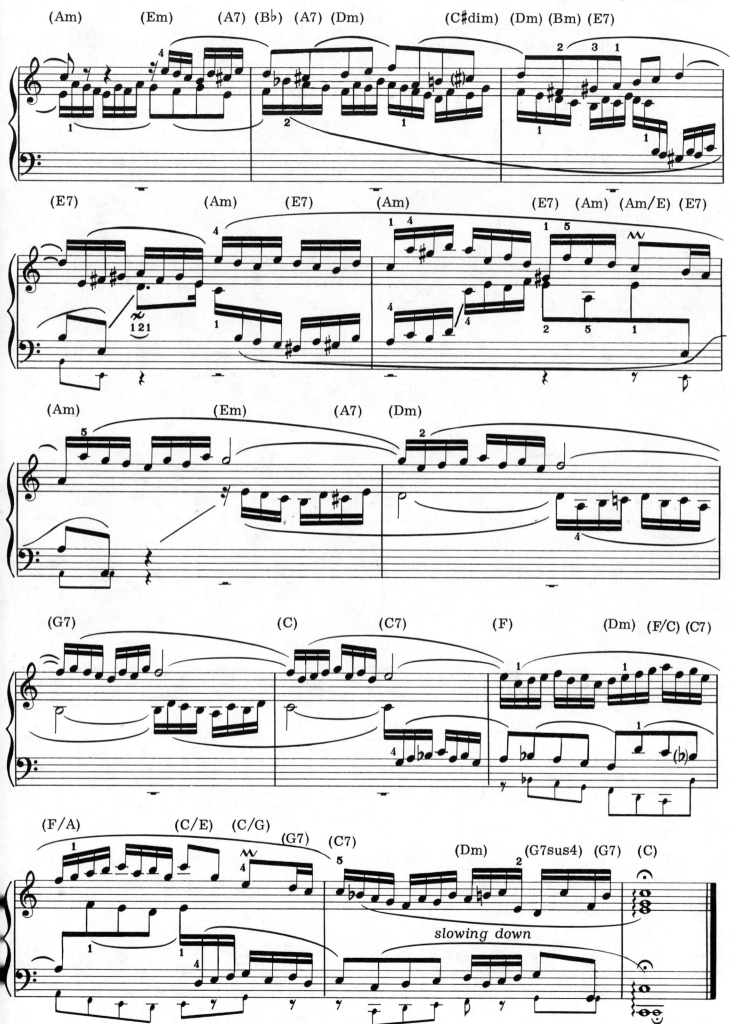

Wolfgang Amadeus Mozart
SONATA IN C
K. 545
First Movement Excerpt

Mozart composed this familiar piano piece in 1788, only three years before he died at age 35—the same year in which he composed his last three symphonies and finished revising his opera *Don Giovanni*. In 1939 Jack Lawrence and Raymond Scott wrote an arrangement of this opening movement, which they entitled "In an Eighteenth Century Drawing Room." The long trill toward the end of the piece should, by tradition, be started on the upper note—that is, E—and played directly on the first beat of the measure.

Ludwig van Beethoven
"MOONLIGHT" SONATA
First Movement

Beethoven dedicated this "Fantasy-Sonata" to the beautiful, vivacious and (most unfortunately for him) already married Countess Giulietta Guicciardi, and the deep melancholy of the piece may very well reflect his feelings at the time. On hearing the opening movement of the sonata for the first time, critic-poet Ludwig Rellstab wrote that it reminded him of the moonlight over Lake Lucerne, which is probably how the sonata received the name we know it by today.

Slow and sustained

Franz Schubert

MARCHE MILITAIRE

In the early years of the 19th century, most well-educated people in Vienna, the world's most musical city, played the piano and sang almost every evening. As a result, there was a huge market for home music, and Schubert, prolific composer and excellent pianist that he was, turned out great numbers of very melodic, graceful and satisfying pieces for amateur pianists.

His three Military Marches, probably written around 1817, are actually easier to play in their original forms as piano duets, but the D major—the Marche Militaire—has become particularly famous in a version for piano solo. One of the most popular precision marches of the famous Lippizaner horses is performed to this music by Vienna's immortal son.

Frédéric Chopin

PRELUDE IN A
Opus 28, No. 7

While sojourning on the island of Majorca for his health in 1838, Chopin completed and sent to his publisher in Paris 24 Preludes that he had been working on. No. 7 of the Preludes (there is one in every major and minor key—see also Prelude in C Minor on page 44) is the A major, a short perfect piece (our arrangement includes the entire work), based on a single melodic theme. It is now familiar to balletomanes as the prelude to *Les Sylphides*.

Johannes Brahms

WALTZ
in A Flat

(Transposed to G)

A century before Brahms wrote his waltzes for piano duet in 1865, the waltz had completely captivated the Viennese, who crowded the ballrooms every night to dance the waltz, and who practiced every day at home the latest sheet-music numbers on their pianos. This famous Brahms Waltz in A Flat, transposed here to G for easier performance, is almost as much cradle song as waltz, effortless in its gentleness and lilt.

Tenderly and gracefully

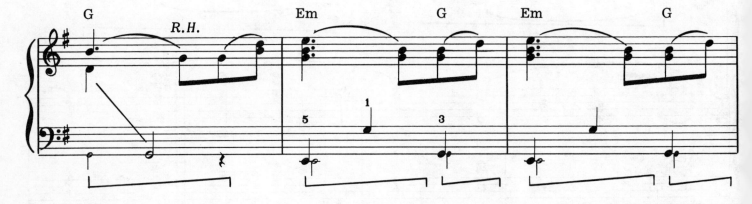

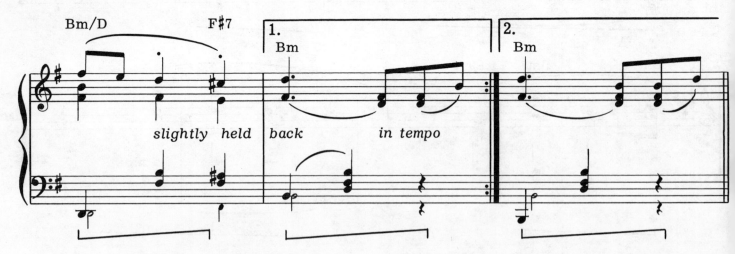

208

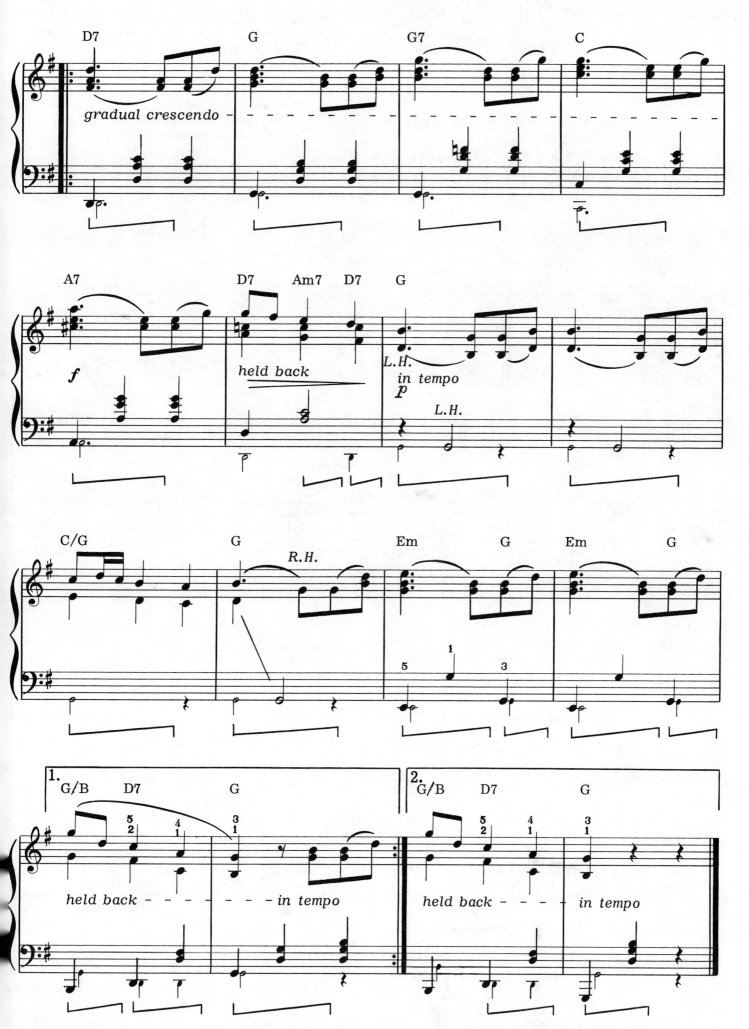

Ignace Jan Paderewski

MINUET IN G

In addition to being one of music's most spectacular pianists, Paderewski was an ardently patriotic Pole. For years he championed the cause of independence for his native country, and, after Poland had been granted freedom in 1918, served as its prime minister. But he was also a great composer of music. His most famous piece is the Minuet in G, which was published in 1899. The "turn," a five-note ornament used on the third beat of the opening several measures, is a major part of the melody's unique charm, and should not be hurried. At the proper tempo, you need not play it very fast, nor should it sound difficult.

Traditional; arranged by Dan Fox
Country Gardens

The Cecil Sharp House in London, which was built and named for the great musicologist, is headquarters for the English Folk Song and Folk Dance Society. Sharp, who hiked all over the British Isles, transcribed, from whoever would sing to him, songs and country dances that had been popular for centuries. He discovered "Country Gardens" in the English county of Somerset. In 1930 the song was popularized by Australian-born Percy Grainger, who published his own showy piano solo arrangement of it.

212

Section Eleven
THREE-HAND ARRANGEMENTS
FOR FAMILY FUN

Johann Sebastian Bach
PRELUDE No. 1
from
"The Well-Tempered Clavichord"

Johann Sebastian Bach • Charles Gounod
AVE MARIA

Struck by the delicate, harp-like figurations of Bach's first prelude in his "Well-Tempered Clavichord," Gounod wrote a corresponding melody, using as words the text "Ave Maria," an ancient church hymn. He orchestrated his beautiful experiment for soprano solo, violin, piano and harmonium. The piece is unique in that Bach's composition is played note for note as it was written, and Gounod's melody is simply added to it. Thus, the accompaniment in our version can be performed by itself, and you will have the original Bach. Add the melody again, and you have vintage Gounod. When the Gounod melody is added, it can be played higher on the keyboard by a "third hand," or on another instrument such as the violin, flute, oboe or recorder. Or it can be sung or hummed by the whole family.

Moderately slow

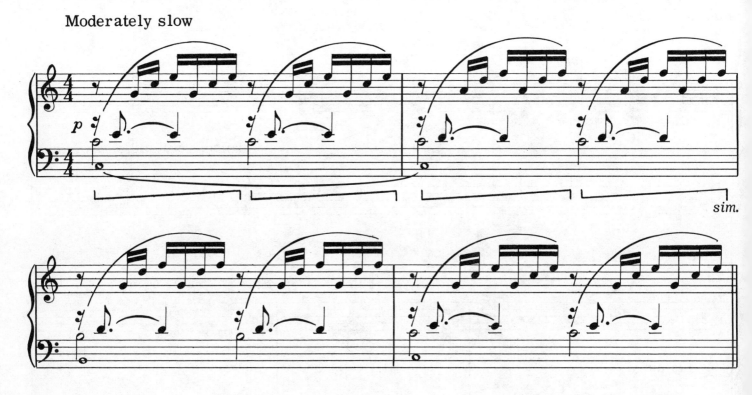

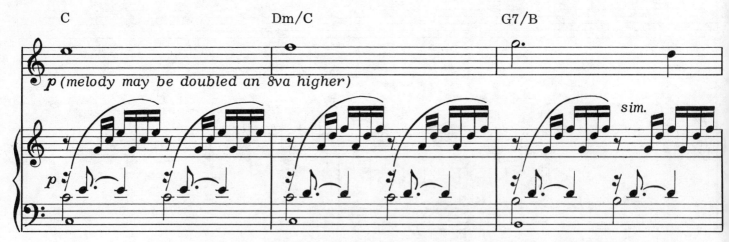

Copyright © 1980 Ardee Music Publishing, Inc.

Giuseppe Verdi

Anvil Chorus from the opera IL TROVATORE

In Verdi's *Il Trovatore,* gypsy men, at work at their forges, sing this song as they strike their anvils with hammers in rhythm. The repeated right-hand notes at the beginning indicate the sparks snapping from the fire; the sonorous strains that follow are the men singing together; and finally, at the key change, the workers pound their anvils as the rhythm broadens to an exciting climax. Any child will enjoy making anvil sounds by striking a fist on the top notes of the piano keyboard. For a more gypsy-like effect, one might clang a few pans and pot lids together. This should be done where indicated ( ) on the second and fourth beats of the measure).

Brightly

Pound fist on top of keyboard.

John Philip Sousa

STARS AND STRIPES FOREVER

The final chorus of Sousa's famous march "Stars and Stripes Forever" features an electrifying piccolo part (marked obbligato) which should be played as brilliantly as possible. The "third hand" can play it on the piano keyboard two octaves higher than notated, or on some other instrument— flute, violin, harmonica, or piccolo, of course. Just don't leave it out if there is another musician available!

Players with small hands may substitute small notes for bass notes throughout.

*³⁄₂ *means strike single key with both fingers for added emphasis. (Not staccato)*

Sousa: STARS AND STRIPES FOREVER

* Third hand at the piano, flute, piccolo, or other melody instrument.
  Add this part on the last repeat only.
** That is, two octaves higher than written.

224

G. H. Huffine

THEM BASSES

G. H. Huffine's "Them Basses" refers not to orchestral double basses or to men with low voices, but to the circus-band tubas which enter after the opening fanfare at every performance. The melody here is assigned to the "third hand" playing the *bottom line*. (Notice, however, that the fingering is for the right hand.) This line can also be played on a tuba or a bassoon, or a trombone (reading the part an octave higher). For a two-handed performance, the player should play the top and bottom staves, omitting the middle staff.

Moderately, in 2 (♩.=1 beat)

Piano

Organ pedal or 3rd hand at the piano (Solo)

Fingering for the right hand.

Section Twelve
SACRED AND CEREMONIAL FAVORITES

Sir Edward Elgar
Pomp and Circumstance March No. 1

Second Theme

British composer Edward Elgar, who was knighted by King Edward VII in 1904, composed numerous oratorios, symphonies and sonatas. Something of a marching-band style is heard in several of his works, especially the six "Pomp and Circumstance" marches. The trio of the first of these, known the world over as "Land of Hope and Glory," is very often played at royal coronation celebrations and at graduation ceremonies.

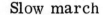

Giuseppe Verdi

GRAND MARCH
from the opera AÏDA

Aïda, which was commissioned by the Khedive of Egypt to celebrate the opening of the Suez Canal in 1871, gave Verdi one of his greatest successes. In the opera, *Aïda,* an Ethiopian princess held captive in Egypt, is torn between romantic love for the Egyptian Captain Rhadames and filial love for her father. As this triumphal "Grand March" is played, the victorious Rhadames and his troops enter the city gates with their prisoners, one of whom is Aïda's father. Today, more than a century after its premiere, *Aïda* still ranks among the world's most popular operas.

Majestically

232

Johann Sebastian Bach

SHEEP MAY SAFELY GRAZE

from "Birthday Cantata"

Bach not only composed religious cantatas for his aristocratic patron in Weimar, where he was church organist for Duke Wilhelm Ernst from 1708 to 1717, but he also turned out ceremonial music as well. In his last year with the Duke (the same year in which he wrote "Jesu, Joy of Man's Desiring"), Bach was asked to compose a birthday cantata for another Saxon nobleman. From the cantata comes a soprano aria, "Sheep May Safely Graze." The accompaniment reminded pianist Percy Grainger of tinkling sheep bells (he called his solo piano arrangement of the tune "Blithe Bells"). The right hand notes are played in Bach's instrumentation by two flutes, which further projects the pastoral quality of the serene music.

Johann Sebastian Bach
Jesu, Joy of Man's Desiring

Bach accepted the position as organist for Duke Wilhelm Ernst not only because it paid a good salary, but because he was concerned about the "betterment of church music." One of his duties was to provide choir music for Sunday services. From one of his cantatas comes "Jesu, Joy of Man's

Desiring," the melody sung by full choir, the wreathing triplet accompaniment played by violins. Our arrangement shows one phrase unadorned, in four-part harmony (measures 9-12), and then as accompanied in Bach's original version by the violin patterns (measures 14-17).

Richard Wagner
BRIDAL CHORUS
from the opera LOHENGRIN

Wagner's opera *Lohengrin* tells the story of the beauteous Elsa and a mysterious knight who appears to champion her cause after she has been unfairly accused of killing her brother. After the knight routs her accusers, he claims her hand in marriage as reward. Blessed as the union seems, it is broken when Elsa defies her husband's bizarre request that she never ask him his name. Revealing himself as Lohengrin, a knight of the Holy Grail, he is sadly borne away from his bride on a dove-drawn boat to his sacred castle. The famous "Bridal Chorus," sung by Elsa's attendants, has probably accompanied more brides up the aisle than any other piece of music ever written. However, though the song's hushed and dignified strains are a perfect prelude to the solemn rite of matrimony, it is sung in the opera after Elsa and Lohengrin have exchanged their vows, not before.

Majestically

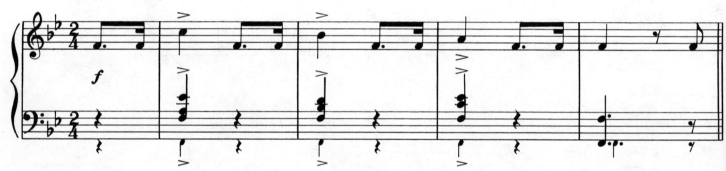

Felix Mendelssohn
WEDDING MARCH
from A MIDSUMMER NIGHT'S DREAM

Mendelssohn was only 17 when he composed his "Overture to *A Midsummer Night's Dream*" in 1826. Then, 20 years later, he wrote several more pieces for a performance of the same Shakespeare comedy, among them the "Wedding March." In the play the march accompanies a triple wedding—the marriages of Theseus and his lovely Hippolyta, and of two other couples who through fairy mischief have previously experienced every romantic tangle imaginable. Today, most newly married couples exit to the strains of Mendelssohn's "Wedding March."

Frédéric Chopin

FUNERAL MARCH
from Sonata in B-Flat Minor, Opus 35

(Transposed to A minor)

In 1836 Chopin composed his famous "Funeral March," which has become the symbol of dignified mourning throughout the Western World. The piece was not published until three years later, when Chopin had written three other entirely different movements and published the whole work as his Piano Sonata in B-Flat Minor. (Our version of the "Funeral March" has been transposed to A minor for easier performance.) The plodding heaviness of the first section should make a sharp contrast to the quietly lyrical melody of the second section.

Slow and solemn

Chopin: FUNERAL MARCH

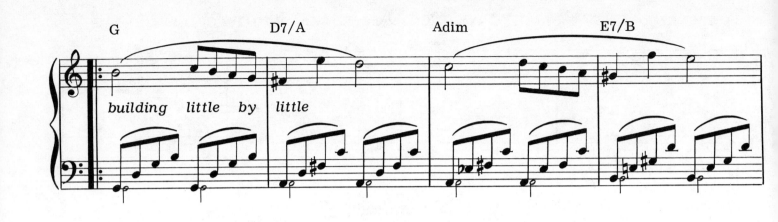

building little by little

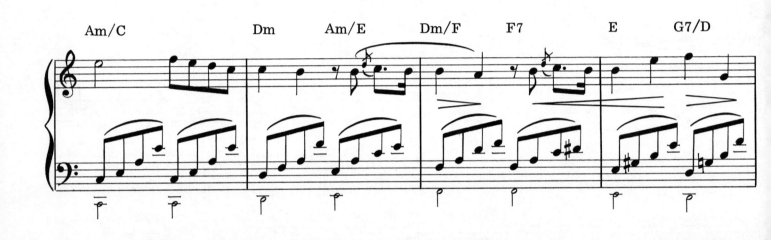

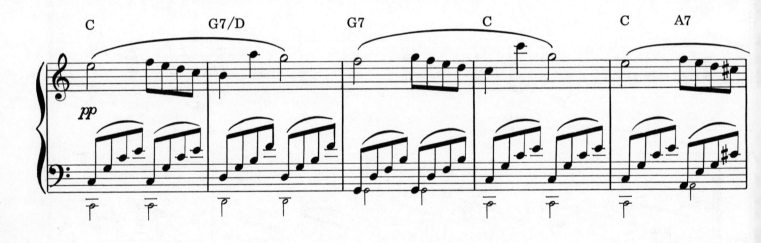

244

Richard Wagner

PILGRIMS' CHORUS

from the opera TANNHÄUSER

"Before I write a verse or a scene, I am already intoxicated by the musical arena of my subject. For my next opera I have chosen the beautiful saga of the knight Tannhäuser," wrote Wagner in 1844. The tale concerns Tannhäuser, a minstrel knight, who deserts his bride-to-be for the allure of sensual pleasures. Finally stricken by remorse, Tannhäuser joins a threadbare band of religious pilgrims and wends his way back to his beloved. As the pilgrims tread their rocky path, they sing this hymn-like chorus of penitence and faith. So beautiful to us is Wagner's opera that it is hard to understand how Robert Schumann could have called it "dull and unnatural, full of crazy ideas, and cacophonous."

Not too slow

Engelbert Humperdinck

EVENING PRAYER
from the opera HÄNSEL AND GRETEL

Humperdinck's opera *Hänsel and Gretel*, which is based on a well-known fairy tale by the Brothers Grimm, was first produced in 1893, and has since become a musical Christmas present for all children. The opera tells the story of siblings who find themselves lost in a deep forest as daylight is fading. Lying down on a bed of leaves, they try to assuage their fright by reciting their bedtime prayers. As they fall asleep, angels from heaven descend on a golden ladder of light to protect them against the evils of the forest.

Moving tranquilly

Franz Schubert

Schubert wrote his famous "Ave Maria" not to the words of the Catholic hymn but to a text from Sir Walter Scott (translated, of course, into German). Ellen Douglas, the heroine of Scott's *The Lady of the Lake* and daughter of an outlawed Scottish chieftain, finds herself not with too few suitors but with too many. When she is about to be forced into marriage with a man she does not love, she appeals for refuge to the Virgin Mary. Schubert's melody combines Ellen's earthly anguish with her trust in heavenly aid. Schubert himself performed his lovely song with his favorite singer, Johann Michael Vogl, at a musical party in 1825.

AVE MARIA

gradually dying away - - - -

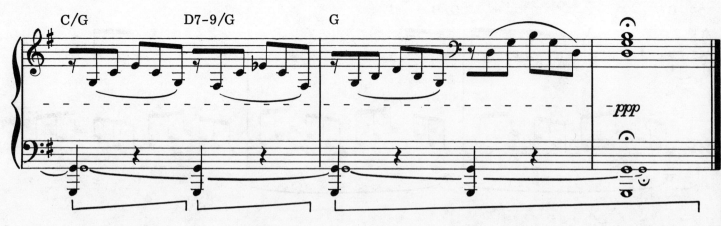

ppp